CRE TIV
HOMEOWN

can't fail room
makeovers

CAN'T FAIL ROOM MAKEOVERS

SENIOR EDITOR	Kathie Robitz
JUNIOR EDITOR	Jennifer Calvert
PHOTO COORDINATOR	Robyn Poplasky
DIGITAL IMAGING SPECIALIST	Frank Dyer
EDITORIAL ASSISTANT	Sara Markowitz
INDEXER	Schroeder Indexing Services
COVER PHOTOGRAPHY	Mark Samu

CREATIVE HOMEOWNER

VICE PRESIDENT AND PUBLISHER	Timothy O. Bakke
ART DIRECTOR	David Geer
MANAGING EDITOR	Fran J. Donegan

Current Printing (last digit)
10 9 8 7 6 5 4 3 2 1

Can't Fail Room Makeovers, First Edition
Library of Congress Control Number: 2008921442
ISBN-10: 1-58011-425-3
ISBN-13: 978-1-58011-425-7

CREATIVE HOMEOWNER®
A Division of Federal Marketing Corp.
24 Park Way
Upper Saddle River, NJ 07458
www.creativehomeowner.com

acknowledgments

We wish to thank our children for enduring a lifetime of turmoil while Mom and Dad relentlessly renovated, refashioned, and photographed every wall and floor around them at all hours of the day and night as they slept on floors, sofas, or makeshift beds. Ten addresses later and still counting, we offer a very special thanks to and for our Max, who could serve as the microwaved hot-dog chef at age 3, and continues today to climb over the project du jour, blithely sweeping the drywall dust from his pillow every night. He is our all-around good sport who has taught us how not to fail, and he has never ever failed us.

A special thanks to Kathie Robitz for her ongoing support and encouragement of Mark's talents, her wisdom in suggesting our collaboration, and her blind faith in Lu's first-ever writing effort.

contents

■ introduction   **6**

■ part 1: *dreaming and scheming*   **9**

the "perfect" room   10
write it down   18
taking inventory   24
balancing the costs   26
five "perfect" rooms   36
plan, plan, plan   46

■ part 2: *architectural elements*   **49**

say hello!   50
distinctive perimeters   60
a change of venue   72
pay attention to the particulars   82
hidden spaces, found places   98
practicality, utility, and delight   116
daily needs   132
vistas, vignettes, and the places in between   148
don't be a dummy   168

■ part 3: *savvy design elements*   **171**

materials that matter   172
good lighting   210
personal color   226
furnishings for comfort   244
collections and displays   260
exclamation points   280

■ resources   **294**   ■ glossary   **296**

■ index   **298**   ■ credits   **302**

introduction

Recently the local home-improvement center moved the store's book section to a new aisle and organized the bookshelves in a horseshoe shape. This new arrangement forms a secluded reading and reference area, making leaning on the cart in a state of design euphoria a little less conspicuous.

If you are no stranger to the thrill of a new and exciting design book, toss *Can't Fail Room Makeovers* into your cart. You'll enjoy the informative design advice and the exploration of renovating adventures precipitated by my own 25 years of experience. In addition, you'll learn the can't-fail techniques and strategies of design professionals, artists, craftspersons, and do-it-yourselfers.

Talking Points

"In the perfect formula, the accent color is just as important as your main color, your smallest piece of furniture/accessory is as important as your main piece of furniture or accessory, the placement of a picture is as important as the artwork itself."

Susan Calabria—Noli Design

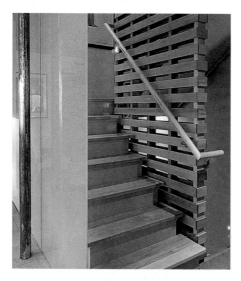

More than a step-by-step guide or reference manual, *Can't Fail Room Makeovers* is meant to set you on your own personalized path of savvy design discovery. It will instill you with confidence that will lead to successful planning methods and decision-making clarity. Whether your design style reflects chic new trends or simplified practicality, your own fanciful flourishes mixed in with some tried-and-true essentials will come together effortlessly in purposeful rooms that will reflect your individuality and creative spirit.

Part 1

DREAMING
and
SCHEMING

- The "Perfect" Room — 10
- Write It Down — 18
- Taking Inventory — 24
- Balancing the Costs — 26
- Five "Perfect" Rooms — 36
- Plan, Plan, Plan — 46

the "perfect" room

Consider these seven key design elements for a can't-fail makeover.

There are a number of distinctive architectural elements in this makeover room that will eventually make it fabulous looking. The **architecture**—millwork, window-seat surround, and windows—set the stage nicely, while the rhythm of the lavender upholstered wall takes the entire room straight to the top.

33

Work with the architecture.

1

Glistening chandeliers and elaborate mirrors reflect the glow of the lovely little brass-and-mirror dressing table. The metal and glass add strength to this decidedly feminine arrangement—exactly what well-chosen **materials** should do. Note that the windows are metal as well, and their black mullions add a dash of the modern and masculine without interfering with the "fancy." The ceiling, which is carefully adorned with gold leaf, is an extraordinary device for one of the most precious materials there is, gold. The subtle pattern, set down by the process itself, adds yet another architecturally rhythmic element overhead.

2 *Choose the right materials.*

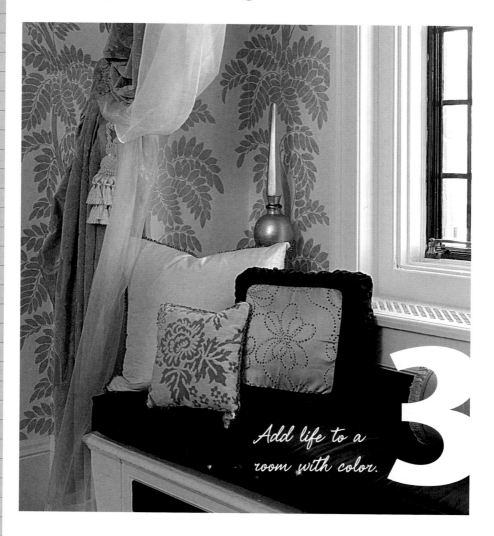

Add life to a room with color.

The wallpaper is "to die for," and the lavender **color** is certainly beautiful. But it is the cobalt blue (see the color swatch, right) at the window seat that gives this room its pulse. It is absolute design genius. Without the blue, the room feels almost monochromatic, and the myriad engaging visuals would be lost to a resting eye. The blue figuratively, and almost literally, pokes you in the eye and gets your pulse racing. I call using such masterful blocks of an unexpected hue "adding punch color." It is a perfect example of how bending a design rule now and again can sound the trumpets in design heaven.

The overall balance of this room is exemplified in the **lighting.**

The opulence of the chandelier supports a lush and indulgent theme. (This idea would also succeed where any boring overhead fixture exists.) On the other hand, the bedside lamp's different style and understated white base lends a collected, less-carefully planned look of informality. The informal table lamp also brings a sense of balance to the elegance introduced by the chandelier.

4

Bring out the best in the room with lighting.

Choose furnishings for comfort and style.

The **furnishings** are actually spare, considering the size of the space, a decision that is further advanced by the airy nature of the chair legs. Because this is no doubt a lady's bedroom, I like the little sexy leg metaphor in addition to the uninterrupted view of the rug.

The room has just a few small **collections,** and the **displays** are under-stated—rightfully so. Restraining the accessorizing to a few well-chosen things keeps this joyously fabulous room from going over the top.

Carefully edit collections and displays.

Add exclamation points.

You will learn in the final chapter of this book that I consider an **exclamation point** as either a focal point, which this room is clearly not lacking, or exactly what the words imply: a subtle but animated form of emphasis—a teeny "tada!" Here, it is the discreet little butterflies scattered on the walls. In this room, which is almost an exclamation point unto itself, it is the designer's willingness for restraint that makes the look so glamorous but, more importantly, believable.

Tada!

write it down

Dream on paper. No matter how large or small your project, start it by making a wish list. Here are nine important things to do when you're compiling your list and dreaming of life after renovating or redecorating.

1 Make a book.

Make your list in an unlined hardcover book, so you can doodle and sketch sudden inspirations or tape in impulsive snapshots taken with a digital camera or camera phone. I like the book to be a wild color and a size that fits in my pocketbook. The color helps me find the book quickly, and because I usually have more than one thing going at the same time, it differentiates one project from another. I generally keep the book in my car so it's always ready when I shop.

Organize the goal.

On the back page of the book, list the seven key design elements discussed on pages 10–17—**architecture, materials that matter, color, lighting, furnishings for comfort and style, collections and displays, and exclamation points.** You should try to incorporate each one into your own makeover room, if that's possible. It isn't necessary to figure out how you might put them together right now. The idea is to refer to the list as you assess the space, with the goal of addressing at least one of these issues during your project.

Walk through and take notes.

With the book and a pencil in hand, begin in your least-favorite room (if your renovations will extend beyond one room), so you'll be less likely to forget about it. You'll also need a measuring tape and someone you love for moral support—and to help with the measuring. Measure everything. Start at the ceiling; measure the perimeter next; then the floor; and finally, the guts.

If you are not sure whether you're going to go for wall-to-wall carpeting or an expensive Oriental rug, just measure the floor. For now, forget about whether you'll use six botanical prints or a large Andy Warhol over the mantel. These decorative details do not matter at the moment. But measure those areas where you know you're going to need "a this or a that" eventually.

Refer to your measurements when you're planning and shopping. For future notations, leave four blank pages at the end of each room's section in the book.

4 Oops! Don't forget.

Go back to each room and note any mechanical, structural, electrical, plumbing, or high-cost carpentry issues that may need to be addressed. Make sure everything works. Look for anything weird, and don't forget things like the door you may need to plane, the piece of trim missing behind the bed, or the electrical outlet that needs attention. Otherwise, I promise you, the door will scratch the new flooring; you won't find the trim paint to touch up "that tiny piece" of trimwork that is no longer hidden by the bed; and you will trip, everyday, over the extension cord that's stretched to the hall outlet powering your laptop.

If you'll be doing a big gut renovation, every interference, outlet, electrical need, and structural or mechanical concern has to be on your plan. If this is too tedious to do at the moment, at least note that there is a problem so you can return to it later. Denial is not an option. There is nothing, and I mean *nothing,* worse than having the roof leak over your beautiful, freshly painted, expensively furnished room.

Plan another day for a basement and exterior assessment of equal detail, even if you're convinced there's nothing to do there. Take the time to be sure.

Take it all in.

Sit in the room for a while. I like to take an empty 5-gallon bucket with me (as my seat), and drag it from corner to corner and all around the space, dreaming and scheming, wishing away. Often a room is planned from the doorway or entry, but the view from the other end is always another thing all together. Get a good feel for the space, in the daytime and at night. Imagine living in the space for a day, and look for any problems that may need to be remedied, which you will note in your book and deal with later in your plan.

Start the doodling for your furniture arrangement ideas, and look for those magazine clippings you've been saving, which can be taped to the walls or in the wish book.

Troubleshoot: what won't work?

Make a list of any conditions, situations, or problems that are interfering with your specific dream for the space. Try not to let a perceived limit drive your design just yet, because you may be able to overcome it in the planning phase. There may be a solution that has not occurred to you yet, or maybe it's in this very book! Just make note of the issue, keep measuring, and go right on wishing.

7

Add purpose.

If you're absolutely sure of the use for your room, go ahead and name it. Define its purpose, and continue jotting down ideas for it. I am working with a client whose king-size bed is in the middle of her living room while a team of contractors renovate her master suite. She genially reported being astounded by how much fun she, her husband, and their two young daughters were having lying on the bed while watching television and reading. Now, I am not suggesting you throw out your furnishings and throw mattresses all over the house, but I am asking you to ask yourself, what level of comfort and decorative device will keep you smiling and your family comfy? Make a list of any conditions, situations, or perceived problems that are interfering with your specific dream for the space, and write it down. Take on the challenge of "it won't work"—extremely outlandish thinking can ignite imaginative solutions that seem less practical at first blush. Working these problems with tenacity and a radical open-mindedness will bring the little glimmers of thought upon which to build. To this thinking, add the tactic of designing by addition or subtraction. Subtractive strategies often yield surprisingly wonderful results, even when a great deal of square footage is summarily lopped off the footprint and dedicated to closets, nooks, niches, or transitions. Similarly, if there is an infringement of some kind, maybe adding on would balance the space. Outlandish thinking takes practice; so keep measuring, go right on wishing, and chances are good that a solution will be clear when you reach the planning phase.

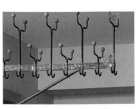

8 *Keep wishing.*

Remember to flip to the seven key design elements now and then, and continue to look for ways to compose your room in a pleasing combination of ways. Would an art collection entirely cover a wall behind the sofa? Excellent! You've addressed three of the design elements at once: architecture, collections and displays, and exclamation points. How will the room be lit? What color will work with the furniture and art that you'll be using? Remember, this is not the time for final decisions—it's for wishing. I wish there was a fireplace; I wish I could paint this room orange; I wish my sofa was a little smaller; I wish I wish ....

9 *Review. How's it going?*

If the wishing is going well, you're likely to have a big list of a lot of stuff you would like buy to put your project room together. Now comes the really hard part. You'll need to start a fresh page. Get the bucket or whatever you've been sitting on; go back to each room; and ask yourself, "What would I really like this room to do? How would I like this room to feel?" Most important of all, ask, "What will make me and all those who will spend time in this room feel really comfortable and happy?"

A happy home is one in which all of its inhabitants can be entirely comfortable being their best. Wish for it; plan for it; and most importantly, be true to it.

taking inventory

Once you've finished a wish list that reflects your design philosophy, it's time to go over what you have, what needs to be changed, and how to get it done. You should find a pleasurable and harmonious way to make everything you love a part of your life—everyday.

1 *Identify what you've got.*

Now it's time to hone down your wish list to things that suit your idea of the good life. To do that, get settled on what you already have, inventory-style. Imagine this part of your project as a movie short or a personal documentary. I suppose you could even do this with a camcorder—a little panning around the room, pointing out the things you love and can never part with, the deal breakers. Everyone in the household will have their own personal wish lists, so allow everybody, including the kids, their voice. Be sure to add all suggestions and requests for a room design or favorite items to the program, while explaining to all that this is not yet a feature film.

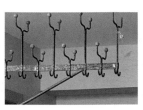

Identify what you can do.

I know this seems odd, but rally the troops. A big project can always use a few extra hands, even if it's to make the coffee and fetch the sodas. Nobody feels left out, and no abilities go unnoticed. Maybe you have really good friends or a close extended family member who can be relied on for help. Friends may have a collection of equipment, tools, or supplies of their own that they may be willing to loan or share. How about a good ladder or perhaps a cement mixer? Don't be afraid to try this; it can save a bundle of money, and you just don't ever know: Uncle Joe might really like to paint, and he might have a dizzying collection of valuable drywall joint knives and 100 rolls of painter's tape hanging around from his own recently completed renovation.

Oh no! This is too much.

Lastly, compile a list that addresses any specialized talent your projects require. These are the jobs that are well beyond your own abilities or those of willing friends and family. Include any professional help you'll need for specific skilled projects, keeping in mind it is more cost effective to upgrade mechanical systems all at once. When your outside labor list is complete, add this information to the wish book, including telephone numbers. Once the overall plan is complete, you can solicit estimates from these contractors. Call them all, one after another; schedule each one to see the project, one after another; wait for the bids; and finish. This limits the agony of getting estimates, which can drag and are a real headache when you're trying to put a budget together.

balancing the costs

Time and money are "kissin' cousins" in the world of home-renovation projects.

By now, you should have a wish list and a solid assessment of your personal inventory. You may be thinking, "Whoa, these chapters are out of order. When does the planning begin? How can I budget when I don't have a plan yet?" Answer: a can't-fail budget strategy is best achieved when the plan is the product of the budget, not the other way around.

There is no point picking out tile for a bathroom that costs thousands of dollars if you only have $500 to spend on the entire room. Besides, good design does not have to cost a gazillion dollars if you incorporate new thinking into the bottom line. If your budget is really tight, you will need to rely a little more on your own expertise and any help you can rally. Can you sew the draperies or paint the walls? Put your own cost-saving talents in the priceless column of your budget. But remember, doing things yourself will usually take more time. Keep strategizing, incorporating some low-cost compromises in exchange for more-expensive quality features. For example, perhaps salvaged materials would make as big a statement as fine millwork.

Anything you already have is free! Look for ways to repurpose or relocate these items. Resist the idea that everything can be done on a dime—every room needs something special. If you're on a limited budget, use your imagination and find the least-expensive, "expensive" something you can get.

Talking Points

"Design is not simply 'creating.' Design is 'listening.'"

Donald Billinkoff—Donald Billinkoff AIA

side-by-side room & cost comparison

Let's take a look at an example of one room with two very different budgets, and see how the art of amalgamation, constantly mixing, blending, and stirring the space and the budget was accomplished by two different owners with two very divergent budgets. Can you tell which is which?*

The room above was five times more expensive.

Architectural Details

The standout architectural detail in each version is the **bookcase** wall. Note how what is in the bookcase is less relevant than the feature itself.

Materials are represented in each room in a nice mix of **textiles** and restrained window treatments. The **hardwood** **maple floor** and the exposed **rough-sawn beam** add the firmness a good natural material suggests. Despite the more gracious quality of the furnishings in the costlier room, the nearly derelict beam adds an interesting texture overhead and does not appear out of place.

Lighting

Both homeowners used the **track lights** on the beam. They "wash" the bookcase and are the answer for evening ambient light. **Lamps** of varying pedigrees are used in each room, and the subtle tie to the pallete is a nice visual rhythm.

Color

This home's site is heavily wooded. A very careful and deliberate balance of interior **wall color** and exterior brightness keeps the room from feeling dark, which in fact, it is. On a sunny day, light appears to fill the room but, even on a cold, gray winter morning, the outside will always appear brighter than the interior—a psychological trick that is explained later in Part 3.

The coffee table in the low-cost room settled nicely into the plan with a quick coat of **chocolate brown** paint. The brown links it to the chair and suggests a modernity that blurs its very humble $5 garage-sale heritage. The **robin's egg blue** paint color used on the high-cost room's ceiling (see pages 32–33) is a nice touch and obliterates the possibility of a green undertone that would come from the reflection of the trees outside. This subtle move also brightens and cleans the space, just as a little bluing brightens up a white shirt. It's a very effective and useful painting device.

Furnishings

In the high-cost room, an overindulgent high-cost stroke of **upholstered wizardry** adorns the ottoman, and yet, doubling as a coffee table helps this handy piece of furniture settle nicely into the surroundings. The ottoman was likely a high-ticket wish-list item, but positioning it in a more featured or opulent arrangement would make the space look out of balance. Both versions of the room are comfortable, thanks to a **convivial arrangement** of a sofa and three chairs.

Collections and Displays

Stylish **artwork,** again advancing the color scheme, is used in each room (see the next page) at a cost difference of nearly ten times, and yet, a similar eccentricity, spirit, and expressiveness are evident in each. Color proves again its ability to bridge the gap for lack of important provenance, while maintaining personality and whimsy. The rhythm and balance in the high-end space are additional architectural assets, but they are not disruptive to the already pleasing perimeter.

Exclamation Points

In the low-cost room, above, the resin **moose head** doubles as art and an exclamation point, no doubt sparking a number of spirited conversations. More artful and careful attention to **accessories** lends a liveliness to the high-cost version on the previous page, with equal panache and a colorful arrangement on the ottoman's tray that announces you have arrived in an awfully great space.

The costs to design this room in its high-end version are approximately five times that of the budget scenario. As to the perimeter, cost is kept very low with the use of an inexpensive "framing" lumber for the bookcase wall. Expert painting disguises this money-saving decision, and the ceiling beam is an affordable dimensional lumber available at any quality lumberyard or sawmill. The overall feeling of the room is serene in both cases, because each version is warm and welcoming, has great proportions, and functions beautifully for a gathering of friends or family. Each of the seven essential design elements is present, making for two equally successful room makeovers. One for a little, and one for a lot.

Stopping the Clock

If your wish list is the ultimate fantasy flight, I regret to inform you that it is now time to return your seat to its upright position. We are arriving at the doorstep of a very unforgiving, unapologetically wily thief indeed, Father Time. Time is a relentless budget buster, and its constant gibe is not easily mitigated by even the most careful management schemes, which are further affected by seemingly endless maladies. Weather, traffic, lost deliveries, lost delivery men, back-orders, miscommunications, injuries, unreliability of every conceivable human and mechanical form, holidays, and tight schedules are some of the things that can cost you, and they are hard to quantify when you are calculating a budget.

Marching On

Careful time management, combined with a commitment to a more realistic and leisurely schedule for the sourcing of goods and services, will pay big dividends on the budgeting balance sheet. Your patience and resolve will allow you to live in a work in progress and leave you with more time to shop, hunt for deals, source some salvage, wait for the busy less-expensive contractors, make good use of your personal inventory, and fine-tune the all-important plan. You will definitely save money, to say nothing of your sanity. Big renovations are inherently disruptive to the most organized households, and walking precariously over drop cloths is the least of it. Factor in every potential scheduling glitch your project may have, and relay them to your entire household with cold, unemotional clarity.

five "perfect" rooms

Before

A flexible floor plan makes good use of space.

Talking Points

"It might be a tired old adage, but on the subject of kitchens, 'Form follows function.'"

Patrick Falco—Falco Design

Before

Talking Points

"The perfect eating room always starts
with a crisp and energetic color choice."

Jackie Higgins—Beach Glass Design

Confident color choices add personality.

dreaming and scheming

Before

Furnish and arrange a room with scale and proportion in mind.

Talking Points

"When designing the perfect room, I always start with a plan."

Marlaina Teich—Marlaina Teich Designs

Before

Talking Points

"It's easy to design when money isn't an issue. But, for the vast majority of us, budget is a concern. Achieving good design within a prescribed budget requires discipline and creativity."

Donald Billinkoff—Donald Billinkoff AIA

Taste and imagination only look expensive.

Before

Simplicity can be a decorating virtue.

Talking Points

"A space becomes special simply by the absence of colors. It can be opulent or classic and allows attention to be paid to every detail. A white room is never forgotten."

Beverly Balk—Beverly Balk Design

plan, plan, plan

To achieve your goals, it's important to have a thoughtful plan.

I've made a big fuss about the plan and I can't stress enough how valuable it will prove to be. But you'll soon agree that the effort you've put into the wish list, the inventory, and the budget, combined with your new-found design savvy, are all going to come together beautifully on a single piece of giant graph paper.

Using the measurements from your wish book, **draw the room to scale.** For example, use a $\frac{1}{4}$" scale, or more simply put, buy graph paper where each box represents 6 inches. Draw the perimeter walls, windows, and doors, and add every permanent feature, electrical outlet, plumbing, and foible. This does not need to be pretty, but it does need to be accurate. List each of the seven essential design elements on the left; note the budget on the right.

Using colored pencils, begin to **place each feature on the drawing.** The colors will make it easier to locate specifics, such as outlets or plumbing. Locate each of your deal breakers on the drawing, and note the corresponding design element accordingly. **List the costs** associated with outside contractors on the budget side, and draw in any work (adding a bookcase, for example) that he or she will perform. **List your personal inventory.** Add anything else that will not affect the budget to the drawing and corresponding element, and do a quick subtotal.

Depending on where your budget is so far, you can plow through to the finish, or begin to mix, stir, and toss the pieces that the game of compromise demands.

Next, **lay tracing paper over the drawing;** put your new-found savvy to work on any issue you noted in the wish book; and begin to dream and scheme an utterly brilliant design solution. If you are not quite there on the budget, hold off on the things that will not affect the structure or enjoyment of the space, but *do not* leave labor-intensive essentials for another day. What has to go and what can't will be easy to figure out, keeping the seven essential design elements in mind, in a descending order of importance: architecture, materials that matter, color, lighting, furnishings, collections and displays, and, finally, exclamation points.

drawing to scale

An informal sketch of the room you are decorating will help you to get a quick idea of what you can do with the space, top. Refine your plans with a formal drawing, which should provide an accurate scaled representation of the room's features and furniture, bottom.

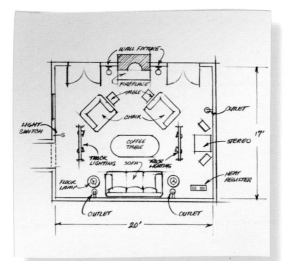

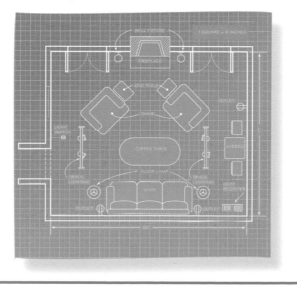

48

Part 2

ARCHITECTURAL ELEMENTS

- *Say Hello!*   **50**
- *Distinctive Perimeters*   **60**
- *A Change of Venue*   **72**
- *Pay Attention to the Particulars*   **82**
- *Hidden Spaces, Found Places*   **98**
- *Practicality, Utility & Delight* **116**
- *Daily Needs*   **132**
- *Vistas, Vignettes & the Places* **148** *in Between*
- *Don't Be a Dummy*   **168**

say hello!

Make a great impression right from the start—at your front door.

"You can tell everything you need to know about a man by the way he plows his field." That mantra, of country gentlemen and serious farmers alike, was something my husband and I learned on our first hay-seeking adventure after we relocated to a rural part of the Northeast where we are surrounded by cornfields and cow farms. Now I can't really claim to know what's different when it comes to comparing cornfields, but I have noticed a great deal of effort is expended on them in terms of precision and neatness. This revelation and its simplicity got me to thinking, "You can tell everything you need to know about a household by the way the entry is kept." That's my own, albeit less time-honored, truism.

Talking Points

"Every home should be a sanctuary: entering it you should immediately feel physically and emotionally protected."

John Saladino—John Saladino Design

A handsome door and hardware says welcome.

Enlarge an entry with a mirror wall.

An immaculate, **art-filled formal entry** implies there are "no shoes or dirty jeans allowed," while a few plants and some colorful, inexpensive area rugs suggests **a more casual atmosphere,** where the dog, the kids, and the guests can come barreling through freely. Give some serious thought to the message you wish to convey, and be very clear; nothing is more disconcerting for a guest than to find themselves standing on Aunt Rose's prized needlepoint rug in muddy boots!

Make it chic with interesting art or a vignette.

Architects and advice-givers of all types recommend creating a reciprocal relationship, a "dialogue" if you will, between the exterior and interior of a home. **Linking them** stylistically and decoratively can be accomplished most simply **with color.** A reciprocal color scheme, no matter how subtle, will begin to suggest from the outside what's happening inside the home. If your interior is destined to be more whimsical than the exterior may otherwise imply, choose a few **punch colors** for doors, flowers, or accessories. Changing the entire exterior color scheme is rarely necessary. After all, whatever drew you to the house you live in initially is probably close to your comfort zone stylistically.

Coordinate the exterior and the interior style.

First impressions and curb appeal not withstanding, **mudroom** and **garage** entries often supersede the more formal front door for all but the most special guests. Entering through a familiar and comfortable **back or side entry** can be an equally welcoming experience, where family and friends are offered a place to pause before or just after entering. More than a place to keep your keys and collect the mail, a good entry is a place for a tiny time-out from the cares of the day, a place to take a minute, and say "hello" to your delightful home.

How you want to live and how you actually live may not be one and the same. The entry is not a good place for ambiguity. Here, the **blissful familiarity** of a family's carefree and casual lifestyle is reflected in a curious yet orderly mix of charming, if somewhat impractical, accessories. But don't be fooled, the acres of cornfields beyond are sown straight as an arrow.

a restyled side entry

Whether it's the front door, back door, or side door, the entrance to your home is the place to formulate an architectural alliance between the outside and inside. This marriage is best accomplished by thoughtful door placement supported by a continuity of materials. To ensure your entrance will stand the test of time and weather, complete your makeover with solid hardware choices and superior quality construction. Here's a good example of how to make a change.

1. The original door placement on this Federal-style house looked odd and thoughtless. It also lacked an overhang, lighting, and a step. Its small size also diminished the overall stature of the house.

2. Enlarged to a full 36 inches and relocated to a better-defined location, the entrance features a new glass door. It is clearly designated as an entrance with a subtle landscaped path and balanced lighting.

3. The bank of windows, while a slight architectural departure, is in keeping with the era. It offers a peek inside that communicates informality and balances the new pergola. The size improves the appearance of the back of the house, and the new door makes carrying iced tea or an afternoon snack to the terrace a breeze.

distinctive perimeters

The treatment of the walls and ceiling will affect the room's mood.

When you walk into your living room with a cup of coffee on Saturday morning, do you look around and think to yourself, "Wow, what a lovely perimeter I have?" Probably not.

The walls and ceilings in a room are surfaces that you **experience** more than **notice** once you live in a space for a while. I've done a fair amount of research on this subject, and there are many complicated psychological explanations for human responses to space. Why do people look up immediately after entering a room? (A quick instinctive check; is it safe?) After taking a few steps into a new surrounding, why do people unconsciously take one step back before planting their feet? (How did I get here? How do I get out?)

These automatic, unconscious responses disappear over time once familiarity is established. Here's how it works: your friends come over, look around, and **observe,** "Wow, this room is so beautiful, you've done such an amazing job! Where did you find those beams? They're amazing." And on a quiet Saturday morning, while the children are still sleeping and the dog is out for a morning sprint, you sit on your sofa sipping your coffee and think to yourself, "This room makes me **feel** so good."

Talking Points

"We need space that liberates us from terra firma, allowing our spirits to soar and our imaginations to take flight."

John Saladino, John Saladino, Inc.

The walls and ceiling are
more than mere backdrops.

Ceiling Savvy

The ceiling is the largest solid expanse in any room, and its height, features, and shape will greatly influence how you feel about the space. For the most part, high ceilings are considered a luxury. This may explain the popularity of **soaring entries** and **two-story great rooms,** or what I call "the cam-corder response," which is a visual reaction as opposed to an emotional one. Over time, however, it can be disconcerting to have so much space above your head, especially in a room designed for sitting or sleeping. The acoustics and noise are difficult to manage, too: high volume above necessitates high volume below. Because living in a noisy house rarely shows up on anyone's wish list, plan beyond first impressions. Lower the edges with a cove or soffit, and follow the form of the roof and windows. This will result in undulating height and forms that create **refreshing visual breaks** that make a room feel intimate and appealing.

Treat a high ceiling in ways that make a tall room feel more intimate.

Open to the rafters, this room is still cozy.

Wonderful Wood to the Rescue

Wood absorbs sound better than drywall, making it a logical material for fixing noise problems. Applied directly to the ceiling surface, wood will modulate the acoustics and add warmth and charm. In combination with paint, exposed wood beams, either as an applied decorative accent or as a structural element, do triple duty, creating **pattern, contrast, and sound absorption**—a great combination. In a hall or entry, where height may be desirable, installing the wood on the walls will do the trick.

Painting wood does little to disguise its inherent warmth and charm. Paneling a wall surface with wood in any sort of configuration is the single most effective way to create a perimeter that **exudes architectural interest.** Such elegance implies a distinctive past when expressed in finely crafted millwork. To some, painting wood surfaces may seem like a terrible idea after all the time and effort involved in crafting these near magical feats of carpentry. But this is where the real magic may begin. Painting stylized millwork, a job to be sure, renders the surface a little more restrained while drawing attention to the pattern, richness, and friendliness of the underlying wood.

The Strength of Stone

For the courageous, a perimeter outfitted with even a single stone wall takes on a strong **character.** Such applications require a lot of planning and can wreak havoc on all but the most unlimited of budgets. Timeless and enduring, the use of stone inside the house is an endeavor that never ends—fireplaces, floors, and walls are the tried-and-true venues for this haughty can't-fail material. Manufactured stone imitators are a reliable and convincing alternative, and the new products have the added benefit of being lightweight. So if you wish for stone, you shall have it—perhaps it is the **most desirable** architectural material of all. Your friends will be chartreuse with envy, and you will have a most pleasing perimeter indeed.

Stone makes a strong architectural statement.

A Distinctive Ceiling

This a fine example of how a good deal of attention to the perimeter renders a room peaceful and very special at the same time. **Decorative medallions** are arranged in a grid pattern and surrounded by simple applied moldings at the ceiling, a low-key profile that is mimicked at the chair rail. A carefully applied coat of white paint in opposing sheens subtly applied in flat on the ceilings and gloss on the moldings enhances the depth of the resulting pattern. This sleight of hand resolves the need for an additional crown or trim **molding** at the ceiling, which would reduce the height and over-complicate the design.

Painting the perimeter above and below the chair rail in opposing colors is not jarring due to the nearly exact matching value of the cool gray and clear beige paint colors. This balancing act of colors renders the perimeter serene.

The monochromatic mural is a mere suggestion, deliberately understated and diffused, while the rug provides a counterpoint to the ceiling arrangement and grounds the room with color. An effect like this can be achieved one layer, or idea, at a time. In your room, you might pare the ideas down to the six individual elements—ceiling, chair rail, color above, color below, mural, and furnishings. Plan out every step of the project, take your time, and remember to start at the top!

Before

Medallions and molding transform a plain ceiling.

distinctive ceiling: before and after

Medallions are available at home centers, art stores, and architectural salvage concerns.

These ceiling moldings are made from a single, plain 1x2 piece of poplar with a routered edge. The joints can be either mitered or butt together, depending on your level of carpentry skill. Use a drop of glue if you join the wood flat, and make the joints as tight as you can.

Before

The mural technique is really just a glorified color wash. Use any leftover wall paint, which can be toned ever so subtly with white, black, or nearly any color paint that you may have. Or check the home center for returned paint that has been marked down. You can also use inexpensive acrylic paint from the art-supply store or a tube of any suitable universal tint.

The area rug makes an enormous color and rhythmic contribution to this room at an affordable price. In a more high-traffic space, as in this room, the furniture placement limits the wear. The size allows for spinning it around from time to time to ensure more even wear, too.

a change of venue

Plain–vanilla staircase? Add interest to this important feature.

Breezing up and down the house is not necessarily an exhilarating experience, unless of course, you have a truly **amazing staircase.** Great architects take great pains to plan an exciting transition from one floor to another, because it really is the only venue where the little kid in everyone comes out to play. However, most grown-ups don't take the fast slide down the rail. This can be a tricky one. Your staircase probably came with your house, and it's a pretty safe assumption the need to tear it out rests somewhere between not really and absolutely not. However, there are ways to increase the architectural integrity of even the most homely little staircase, so let's go!

A staircase in an entry hall makes an immediate style impression.

Flights of Fancy

Current trends for **stairs** and **railings** specify oak treads and risers, and a balustrade of painted spindles, or balusters, and a complementary wood handrail stained and waxed to match. No question about it, this will get you where you need to go. The least-expensive and effective way to **personalize** stairs and boost their architectural impact is with paint. If you have a small older staircase—which, if new, probably would not meet today's fire codes—preserve it. You can treat it to all sorts of imaginative displays. More formally placed central staircases will benefit greatly by adding color to the risers. **Painting the spindles** or **staining the rail** a darker tone will also increase the contrast and rhythm of even a very ordinary stair configuration. Be sure to remove every bit of wax from a handrail before you perform the transformation. Stains and paints will not adhere to a waxed surface.

Talking Points

"There is no excuse for doing anything which is not strikingly beautiful."

William Morris

Add personality to stairs by
combining paint and stain.

The Newel Post

A very satisfying transformation can be achieved by changing just the rail and balustrade or updating the newel post. An **oversized** newel post will act as a nice landmark, grounding the stair at the point of arrival while offering something substantial to grab on to for the final spin. This falls somewhere between leaving it alone and tearing it out. Do a little investigating before you reach for the sledgehammer; there is often a threaded metal rod inside the newel post of an older home. Check it out from the floor below, and if you feel the need to surrender, maybe simply adding a really **unusual finial** will do the trick. The finial pictured here is actually a copper buoy, perfectly aged from years marking a channel on the Hudson River. An oversized drapery-rod finial or an **architectural salvage** find in a similar scale would also work, and if it falls off now and then, rent the movie "It's a Wonderful Life."

Replace or refurbish the newel post.

Along the Way

Outfitting the walls with **artwork** will tie the trip up and down together rather nicely. A visual link will create continuity between floors and designate the spaces for both arrival and departure. Such subtle cues subliminally create a visual "room" **at each level.** Each one becomes a place to stop for a minute, get your slippers on right, or reach for a tiny hand.

Line the wall next
to the stairs with art
or photographs.

*Make one wall
a special feature
with color.*

A Place to Arrive

A coat of **vibrant paint color** on the high wall, which stretches from floor to floor, will keep you company on the trip. The color will serve an equally practical purpose when the tiniest hands in the house grow a bit and begin the maddening if understandable practice of tracing elaborate shapes along the wall, sometimes with crayons. Paint this wall a super durable, washable, and easy-on-the-eye color that you don't mind going over with a damp cloth now and again.

a cost-saving staircase rehabilitation

The stairs pictured here are 200 years old, and therefore easy to forgive for the sag and creaks of such longevity. While it looks humble, the staircase may have a distinguished history—the chestnut wood treads were simply painted over the years, apparently first an oxblood red, then green, then red again. There was some evidence of blue, and some consideration was given to revealing the underlying wood.

Stripping old lead paint is never a safe or easy task, nor is sanding old paint a particularly advantageous alternative. In the end, the state of disrepair belied the structural soundness and history won out.

With a gentle lift of the jack, some labor-intensive wood filling, a very light sanding, and an application of state-of-the-art primers and paints, the grand old staircase was rendered pretty again. Note that it was never quite beautiful, but rather a sound and utilitarian example of early nineteenth-century construction. The sturdy old cherry newel post is original, and the handrail remains as it was found, cleaned and polished with a fresh coat of tinted wax, and ready to steady the hands of the new owners, who love it just as it is.

pay attention
to the
particulars

Little things mean a lot when you want to make a room special.

I t is often said, "God is in the details." It's just as often said, "The Devil is in the details. Period, the end," as my dearest friend, Peter, says. So which is it? Let's avoid this controversy and agree that one thing is for sure: it's always the little things, which I call "particulars," that cause the most commotion.

The big decisions require thought or at least a family conference, but when it comes to the little things, most of the time you're on your own. You return from an impulsive left turn with what you believe is the most **unusual, wonderful,** and **fabulous** something. Trust your instincts, because these little things are where your **true spirit** can shine when expressed in a genuine, if sometimes curious, fashion. Who cares if it's too big if it really makes you happy?

Group similar objects, shapes, colors, or materials.

The Answer on Quantity

Anything, and I mean anything, displayed or assembled in unusual quantity creates rhythm. Because **rhythm** is an effective architectural device, it offers a lot of bang for the buck. Extraordinary quantities of ordinary items appear whimsical. Anything that will set a guest and family member to wondering, "How'd you stack that up? How long did it take to find all those things?" You get the idea. Elicit a lit-tle wonder from **unpredictable personal expressions.** While not necessarily on the top-ten list of architectural details, wonder creates a **good vibe** in a house and piques the interest of even the most casual observers. Guessing how many eggshells are in the vase will be a memorable puzzle to the visiting little league team, who will give no thought whatsoever to the why of it all.

*Create art out of
the ordinary.*

Fresh fruit makes a luscious table display.

Quirky collections can be charming.

architectural elements

While a spare room can look severe, too much clutter is distracting. It's like listening to two songs at the same time—you can't quite get the beat of either one of them. A good **edit** will settle things down. Keep in mind that **pairs** work beautifully, and **repetitive** details or similar objects grouped in an orderly arrangement will have the same pleasing effect. Chances are good that if you have a room that's just a little "off," all it needs is some rhythm to make it sing.

Repeated themes or objects can add wow.

A tight grouping of numerous framed prints gives the impression of just one.

The theme appears to be squares.

In Pairs, or Just One?

Singular displays make an equally **memorable** statement. This is an obvious play on quantity, which again slows things down visually, creates pattern and order, and is a **clear** and **simple** display of form. These concepts are expressed here in a singular, perfect design element, the calla lily. Any form worthy of your consideration will benefit from being showcased center stage and **all alone.**

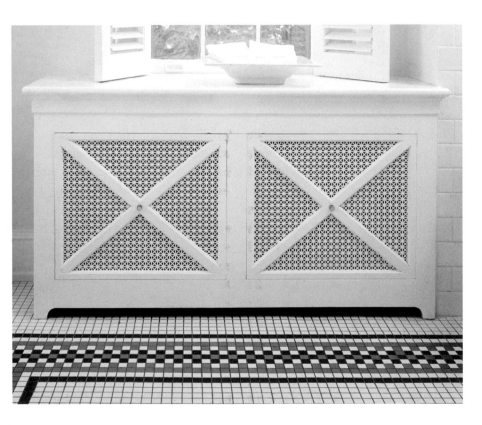

Talking Points

"After the design is firmly fixed, the decoration is added. Decorating is the final enhancement."

Albert Hadley

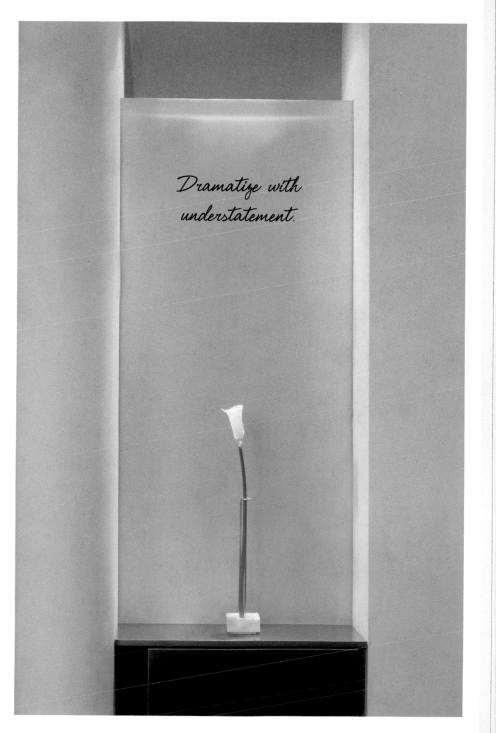

Dramatize with understatement.

The Wisdom of Age

A little age can be a source of great pleasure around the house. Like a wonderful story, the who, what, when, where, why, and how of anything that has been around awhile will fill imaginations with all manner of speculation and fuel the senses. Who owned this thing? Why does it smell like candy? What do you suppose it does? Stories and **conversation, curiosity,** and **wonder** all are expressed in a funny little mirror once used to make bricks or a giant old tobacco mural rescued from the side of a barn. The wisdom of age, "Period, the end."

Vintage objects tell a story.

Rescued or salvaged items add character to a home.

hidden spaces, found places

Nooks, crannies, and other compact storage and display spaces may already exist in your home.

There is a place in every house that's hidden from plain sight and requires no painting or special finishing. It quietly and modestly performs its essential tasks—keeping the wires and holding up the ceilings. It is represented on an architect's drawing by two close, perfectly straight lines that I dutifully and carefully stay within when planning important rooms. I like this space a lot, and wrack my brain seeking ways to exploit it with obsessive determination. So where is this elusive place on the plan, where folly and genius commiserate to ruin my pencil leads? It's between the walls.

In the kitchen, extra shelving is always handy.

Backing Into Space

A typical 16 x 20-foot room with an 8-foot ceiling has approximately 567 square feet of perimeter walls, minus doors and windows. But here's a secret: **between the walls,** assuming they are constructed with 2x6s, there is at least 64 cubic feet of raw space. It's not a lot, but hey, it's not really doing much anyway (except maybe holding up the house), so why not put it to good use? The spice cabinet in this kitchen was created by backing into a typical interior wall. A standard 8-ounce spice bottle measures 2 inches in diameter, so you can see how many of them you can store in this **hidden niche.** And by installing the door in a picture-frame overlay style, you can free a tiny bit more depth.

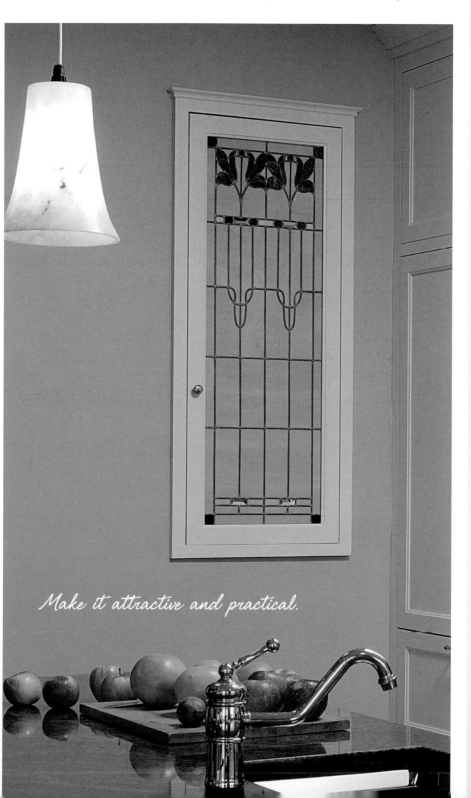

Make it attractive and practical.

Look What I Found

Get that unwieldy vacuum hose out of the front closet by creating a specific space for its storage. All it takes is about 9 inches, found for the example here within a thick timber-framed 12-inch wall. By extending the depth of the space beyond the standard 6 inches, we gained the additional room needed to accommodate a **bookcase**

niche. Trimming the entire wall as a built-in element blurs the fact that it is simply found space inside a wall. Wires run below, inside the lower portion that has been thoughtfully finished with white-painted bead board.

Adding a little light and using glass for shelving would up the ante of these small nooks. Take the time to **plan carefully,** measuring the display pieces, and dreaming up imaginative compositions for light rails, trim details, and doors.

Find innovative ways to make use of dead space.

Miniature Spaces

Deliberately planning spaces that appear carved out of a wall result in a custom look. These niches are especially useful in a bathroom, when a corner or a nook can add desirable privacy. Bookcases, cabinets, display shelves, and ledges all make attractive use of limited space. Playing up and carving out **"negative" space** is an effective architectural trick, but don't overdo it. Removing existing framing will require headers and structural supports, so leave them in place.

Build units into a knee wall or crawl space.

*Floating shelves
and lighting
become an
architectural
feature.*

Use small spaces to create a custom design.

Talking Points

*"Architectural focal points give a space a feeling of
vitality and permanence."*

Andreas Letkovsky—Andreas Letkovsky Architecture P.C.

Adjustable shelves let you change the display with ease.

Use a niche to break up a large wall.

*Convert a closet into a pantry
with a pocket door.*

A Little Closet Savvy

It's hard to conceive **giving up closet** space, but what is a closet really? It's often just a few poorly planned shelves with a less than exciting door. (There is more about this in "Daily Needs," page 132.) Put on your thinking cap, and dream and scheme the night away. Remember, you're not giving up a closet, you're gaining a "something." It might be a something on your wish list—a **pantry** or a tiny **office,** for example. So here's an excellent opportunity to make that wish come true.

Closet doors are another convention with which I take issue because doors imply privacy, a message that guests may wrangle with in the powder room when they are looking for a towel. **Removing a closet door** will create a friendlier open place, where a guest will feel free to grab a fresh towel or a new bar of soap. This may seem a little radical, but think about the last time you felt like a snoop in someone's house hunting for a new box of tissues. Simply leaving closet doors open can also be very charming. For any open closet notions, try painting the doors a swell color or replacing a standard door with shutters. Open closet spaces stay organized and clean, add visual appeal, and can be outfitted in a more versatile fashion.

Replace a standard door with something different—shutters, for example.

Remove the door—but only if your closet is reasonably tidy.

a unique way to use negative space

A 40 x 108-inch "negative" wall was outfitted with shelving that was designed for practical and display purposes. The dimensions of the shelving match the intended contents of the storage and display areas. A salvaged horse-stall door began an exciting dialogue, which was echoed throughout the kitchen's renovation. The pattern of the rusted ironwork is mimicked in the grid of the nearby pantry cabinets, while the chevron motif of the lower door area was repeated at the mudroom door. The aged, horse-kicked, painted-here-and-there wood door adds charm and a nice mix of materials that offset the newness of the remodeled room.

1. The door was installed on a door trolley similar to that of it's horse-stall origins. It allows the door to glide effortlessly in front of the diminutive space and solves the problem that a swinging door would pose in a small area. This way, the door sits nicely over the jog when it's open.

2. Simple trim details conceal the galvanized door trolley and turn the entire area into a single, cohesive architectural element.

3. The finished project forms a delightful little interlude in between the kitchen and dining rooms, and it defines the equestrian interests of the homeowner.

practicality, utility, and delight

Organize your home to suit your family's needs and lifestyle. One size does not always fit all.

When I was a young child, instead of watching cartoons in the morning, I would circle the kitchen with a little metal lunch box hoping to hear my mother say in her sing-song fashion, "You're going to work with Daddy today!"

My father owned a small appliance and television repair shop where there were tall stools to sit upon, teeny-tiny tools to play with, and what seemed like a gazillion things in need of sorting. These were little things, and my favorite was something called "capacitors." They looked a lot like unusually colored Good & Plenty candies with three to five little wires sticking out of each end.

So on the best days of all, I'd sit on a tall stool and sort capacitors by color and wire configuration, while my father tinkered with televisions and toasters, taking time out now and then to mention what an excellent organizer I was and to share his pastrami on rye with extra mustard and a Funny Bone, please, for dessert.

The value of **organization, precision,** and **order** is immeasurable in a home. Function is "order of the highest order," accomplished when scissors and the dog's leash are as easy to find as a cold drink. It's something that can be acquired with or without the aid of a good pastrami sandwich.

Thoughtful design makes organization easy.

Practicality in the Kitchen

Be true to yourself and your household when making organizational decisions for the kitchen. Keep practical needs in mind. The most beautiful kitchen is an utter functional failure if there is no place for the trash. Kitchens tend to become dumping grounds for all kinds of miscellany, so plan accordingly.

To function well, the kitchen has to meet the needs of the entire household and everyone's lifestyle. **Recycling, composting, buying in bulk,** and **cooking fresh foods** brought in from the back garden is a different **lifestyle choice** from dining out nightly or entertaining a house full of guests for sushi on a Saturday night. If you have children, plan a place where they can reach the things you allow them to fetch for themselves. Of course, get the cleaning solutions out from under the sink. Other can't-fail kitchen ideas include organizing an area for specialized cooking, making the most of wall space with **attractive shelving,** and planning the largest **pantry** possible.

*Make use of every
square inch of space.*

Talking Points

"Designers can effect a lot of change by producing things that are elegant, beautiful, and efficient, whether they're interiors or buildings or products."

Cindy Coleman

Locate items where you will use them.

Practical ideas can be pretty.

A pantry can be a separate room...

A Dream Pantry

More than sorting capacitors in my youth, years of successful kitchen planning has rendered me a certifiable organizational zealot. For example, I know that most boxes of breakfast cereal measure 10 inches and that the big boxes are 11 inches, except for the Cheerios, which are 11½ inches. So 12 inches works for cereal storage.

Canned soups of any kind **fit on a shelf** that has a 6-inch clearance, but if there is 7 inches, four 1⁹⁄₁₆-inch cans of tuna will stack neatly on the same shelf. Most crackers fit in a standard stock cabinet drawer, but if you eat a lot of Cheez-Its, you'll have to store them elsewhere because they come in 9-inch boxes.

A standard full-height pantry cabinet, which has shelves that you can place to accommodate your boxes of dry foods, will yield more storage space than you think. So **organize by container size,** and space the shelves accordingly with 2-inch clearances.

...or it can be a tall built-in cabinet.

Delightful Utility

There was a time when every new-home floor plan designated a space for something called the **"utility room."** The laundry, possibly the water heater, and a ladder were generally stored in this windowless dead end off the kitchen, and it was a dreary spot indeed. Today's new homes often provide the mudroom and a separate laundry room. Rather than a sacrifice, giving over a lot of space for the utilitarian demands of a modern lifestyle goes far beyond basic utility.

Talking Points

"The most important functions of a building are its human uses."

Andre Dubus

A bright spot makes everyday tasks less of a drudgery.

Can't Wait Until Laundry Day!

In an older home without a good laundry setup, don't hesitate to steal a room if it's possible. Why not put the laundry behind the closed door of a front room if you never use that space anyway? Don't settle. Design a laundry room that suits your family's specific needs, and make it a pleasant place to spend time, too.

If there is a **pretty spot** with a window, make it a little fancy with good counter surfaces and water- and energy-efficient **front-loading machines.** Often a loyalty to an old top-loading machine is the only thing standing in the way of a better laundry room.

Here, the expense of adding a beautiful window is balanced by the low cost of the countertop material, slab pine, which is stained an invigorating orange to look clean and bright.

Front-loading machines save work space.

Command Central

Every home needs a command center. This is not an office. Nor is it "the top drawer in the kitchen." It is a place where there is always a telephone and emergency numbers are at the ready. There should also be a pen, some paper, a few dollars, and maybe a roll of tape in one of the drawers. This is where to run when the cat drinks your afternoon martini (call poison control) or the delivery guy warrants a tip (it's in the drawer). This could also be the place you'll be absolutely sure to find at least five extra pairs of reading glasses next to the basket of mail.

Plan it, no matter how small or how large, with the same attention to detail you would extend to organizing a trip to the Mojave Desert. Give it a name so that everyone in the household will know the scissors are in the drawer at "Command Central," or whatever you want to call it at your house.

A small desk in the kitchen is usually adequate.

A computer makes it a communications hub.

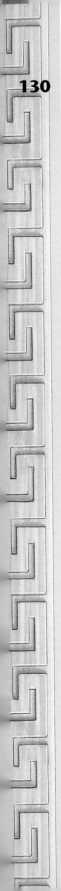

planning a command central

According to my son-in-law, "The Kernel" of Kernel Computer Services, there's an awful lot I don't know about computers. No, I've never been to a genius bar or talked to anyone on the Geek Squad. I simply call "The Kernel" when there's trouble. But I do know something about setting up a command central at home. And although my children think my rotary phone is nostalgic, they admit that they would be in trouble after a few hours if the power goes out and their cell phones need charging. So here's what I think it takes for an efficient command central.

1. Emergency numbers and a hardwired **"always-there phone"** that doesn't need a charge. It's not that nostalgic, I promise.

2. As a general rule, new electrical devices often require grounded three-prong receptacles. It may be necessary to do some new wiring. Creating a wiring chase behind a cabinet, which was done for the installation, here, may be the simplest method. According to "The Kernel," up to six devices can be plugged into the strip, and it's handy for charging the cell phone, the BlackBerry, and the iPod.

3. An old-fashioned pen and paper (I can't believe this), **stamps, calculator, scissors, a place for keys,** and all of the little conveniences of the day.

4. Batteries, candles, matches, and a flashlight. Hunting around for these things in the dark is harder than you think.

Bulletin boards, calendars, message pads, a box of crayons, and coloring books for an unexpected young guest, your **vitamins, a few band aids, a measuring tape, rubber bands,** and my personal favorite, **a straight razor** (which proves to be very useful when it can actually be found), are a few more items a command central could keep handy.

daily needs

Keep everyday items nearby and attractively on display.

This chapter is about something that is rarely the subject of a professional photographer's perfect picture making. So far, you have been enjoying many fine images produced by a dear friend and architectural photography genius, my husband, Mark. Assisting him as a photo stylist now and then, I have had the opportunity to spend time in many beautiful homes and see how other talented designers tackle demanding renovations. As the stylist, my job is to make the rooms ready for their close-ups, placing flowers here, moving a chair there, and removing all the stuff great photo editors never want to see—what I call, "the daily needs." But there are ways to make even the most mundane items look attractive.

An organized closet is a beautiful thing!

Soaps and lotion bottles can spruce up a plain bath.

Where's the Toothbrush?

No matter how well displayed or thoughtfully **organized,** toothbrushes, sponges, dishes on the drain board, scrub brushes in the shower, towels to dry wet dogs, and an entire category of its own, kid stuff, all have to disappear before a "perfect" room is photographed. Haven't you ever asked yourself, after leafing through a design book or a magazine, "Do people really live like this?" Most do not, but along the way, I've discovered some tricks and ideas for those who almost do. In other words, there are ways to keep the **little necessities** handy and attractively displayed.

Bath ensembles for the vanity can carry out a design theme.

You can find vintage bottles on the Internet or at antique shows.

Quantity Can Equal Quality

In "Pay Attention to the Particulars," on page 82, I suggested that exuberant and whimsical displays were culled from rather ordinary items. Further alchemy can be fashioned out of the potions of a daily shower when a spot is designated for **pretty bottles,** soaps, washcloths, towels, and brushes. It helps when the bottles and soaps are interesting or an unusual **punch of color.** (See how this is all coming together?) While expensive soaps and lotions may prove taxing to the budget, a **nice container** is a nice container. Find one, and fill it with something swell looking and affordable. Choose just a few coordinating indulgences to mix with the basics. Ramping up the quantity of even the most utilitarian things will make for some awfully pretty pictures.

Flaunt your stuff!

Honor Your Passions

If you can spare the space, designate an entire room to a passionate pursuit, or consider working a hobby into a **themed design.** While themed rooms have terrible reputations at the moment, trying to hide the amount of stuff such passions amass can be another problem. Certainly, the baseball enthusiast's accumulation that is showcased here (opposite bottom) is well beyond the bounds of the ordinary. It certainly justifies an entire room. Think about how much closet space it would consume. The semantics of this can be misleading at any rate; after all, what exactly makes a room a room and a closet a closet?

Incorporate a hobby into your design.

Put your passion on display.

A large walk-in closet can
change your life—almost!

Speaking of Closets

I know, I know, and I'm sorry, really, but everyone needs a dream, no? A really over-the-top, super-organized, unbelievably beautiful closet is pretty high up on my list, so why not at least consider the options. Affordable **closet systems,** which make a high level of organization possible, are now readily available though a number of online vendors. One company ships all the pieces "flat packed," with clear instructions, user-friendly components, and a simple design program for scheming and planning on its Web site.

Closet organization will definitely help rev up things in the morning—no more last-minute searching for the right shoes. The kids will benefit, too, when putting away their own laundry becomes a straightforward, easy-to-follow program. As is true of the kitchen pantry, a similarly well-planned closet utilizes limited space most efficiently. For casual wardrobes, consider **grouping** the entire household's long hanging clothing together in a single, perhaps special closet that's not necessarily in a bedroom. Sunday's best and dry-cleaned finery will stay cleaner and neater stored safely and neatly out of the way, while freeing up space for everyday shirts and jeans.

Now you see it, now you don't.

A closet system
can cater to
your needs.

Even a shoe collection has aesthetic merit.

Be artful in the way
you address daily
necessities.

Mind the Little Things

In "Hidden Spaces, Found Places," beginning on page 98, I talked about the space inside the walls. Here's another example, on the opposite page, this time for a hodge-podge vase collection and a **unique** water dish station for the dog. If you have a pet, and know that you're always going to have one, consider some solutions for their housing and daily needs, too.

Tripping over the dog dish can be averted with a little **ingenuity.** Remember, what's happening in your household each day can be as effortless or carefree as your inventiveness and design savvy allows. Why not spend a little time overcoming unnecessary annoyances, and when you do, would you mind terribly sending along a nice picture?

Talking Points

"Nothing is in good taste unless it suits the way you live. What's practical is beautiful...and suitability always overrules fashion."

Billy Baldwin

Ah, the Television

If the goings on around my house are any indication, it's a safe bet that despite the advent of nearly pencil-thin plasma screens, the **great television debate** continues to rage. Did you ever think a TV in every room and a room for every TV would really happen? (I'm still looking for the chicken, but that's another book.) There seems nary a space where devilishly small plasmas won't fit, and the deceptively big ones are, shall we say, really really big. While thinness is definitely a plus, the most diminutive TVs, which fit in the most unlikely places, take multitasking to a whole new level. To friends I'll admit that yes, I like a little Oprah in the kitchen. On the other hand, as a designer in a constant search for the Holy Grail of **television storage,** I do have some rules and thoughts, which are by no means hard and fast, and in no particular order of importance.

When it comes to TVs, thin is in.

Design a cubby in the kitchen for a small TV.

my rules for tv space

1

1. Forget about trying to hide it. It's just too big.

2. Plan the wiring into any room makeover, even if you don't own the TV just yet. These pesky teeny tiny televisions are very seductive and fit in the most unlikely places. Plan for more than one; they're like rabbits.

2

3. Consider that next year, another 6 inches may be required in the previously allocated, seemingly enormous amount of space. Be very sure when you're making a commitment to an overly extravagant, high-cost, built-in cabinet. And for some reason, the smaller the TV, the greater the price.

vistas, vignettes,
and the
places in between

Frame the view to interesting interior and exterior spaces.

Windows are the single element that architecturally defines a house. No matter what the renovating program, windows are where the real paralysis sets in and the second guessing starts with a vengeance. "Maybe we do need an architect." "Why do they make so many different kinds of windows"? "Why won't any window fit into this opening?" Then there's "Wait just a minute there, Sally, how much is this going to cost?" For a can't-fail renovation that will involve changing a number of windows, I strongly suggest a good alliance with a reputable window and door dealer, builder, design professional, or architect. Fenestration, or more simply put, the arrangement of windows in a house, is definitely big doings. Even replacing existing windows can be a daunting task, best accomplished with some professional advice beyond what you will read here. I can, however, suggest another approach to planning and successfully accomplishing a no-less beautiful improvement in your home.

Dramatic window sizes and many different styles are readily available today.

Creating Vignettes

There is something inherently satisfying about a view that demands your attention, especially if it is framed in such a way as to form a **vignette.** These "punch windows" invite a peek, but they generally demand the favor of a bend, a tippy toe, or a deliberate pause in exchange. The **reward** is as much in the pause as the view, so don't concern yourself too much with exactly what is on the other side.

Glass is as much about decoration
as it is about the view.

A window seat can be a comfy nook.

Window treatments filter light and add privacy.

*Interior glass doors extend
natural light inside a home.*

This interior vista was created to draw attention to the art.

Careful Composition

Framing a view into a room or even a piece of the room beyond is no less captivating than an unexpected glimpse of the outdoors. Such **interior portals,** or framed compositions, add character to a house by virtue of their restraint. More surprise than drama, the ability to additionally open and close the view with doors now creates a sort of architectural peekaboo that lends a comforting coziness to either side of the visual game.

Framing the entryway from room to room with cased openings trimmed in contrasting paint colors is another means to **visually narrow down** the approach, blur the references for ceiling heights, and balance the scale of spaces with tall or vaulted ceilings.

Architecurally strong trim elegantly frames the view into this dining room.

Multiple doorways frame a view to a dramatic fireplace.

The Perfect View

The most effective example of a vignette is one in which the view is not only framed, but goes on to terminate at a window. This rare and **delightful composition** is the architectural equivalent of a home run, which should never ever be overlooked. Seize any opportunity for vignette and vista to form an **incredible collaboration,** and enjoy the view from what is likely to become your favorite spot in the house.

Tall windows bring the outdoors inside.

Large pendant fixtures create visual
pauses in a long hall.

Talking Points

"Good design has to tell a story. It has to stop people, and it has to make them wonder."

Zahid Sardar

Along the Way

In a well-designed house, getting from room to room happens in **halls and transitional spaces.** Careful attention to the view afforded by the destination room and enhancing all that happens along the way is a worthwhile pursuit. Too often painted a neutral color and outfitted with a simple lighting element, boring halls become mere corridors, rendering the spaces on either end of them jarring. If the hall is unusually long, framing another opening, even if the opening is essentially in the middle of the hall and neither framing or designating anyplace in particular, will give the eye some visual reference while creating more desirable **architectural continuity.** Cohesive and firm, interesting hallways that are a visual delight can trick the most astute spatial observer into thinking, "Wow, this place goes on and on!"

Watch Out for Grandma

Old houses and many small ones do not have the benefit of **contemplative places** in between rooms that can be filled with visual reward. In these homes, creating an exciting view now and then will open the home visually and offer endless opportunities for architectural interest. Vintage or period homes are usually very accepting of window seats, interesting punch windows, and subtle departures when they are carefully designed.

However, the easiest can't-fail suggestion is to install **glass doors** where there are existing windows. The doors do not have to lead to anywhere special, but if they do, all the better.

A dormer window offers an opportunity for adding a window seat.

French doors can replace an old window.

An equally effective proposition might be to frame an existing, but well-defined, space with **new windows.** Think breakfast area, laundry room, attic bedroom—preferably someplace that will not interfere with the existing facade or elevation too much. In a modest Cape Cod-style house for example, a departure from an existing double-hung window might introduce a casement unit, but still maintain a similar light pattern. Repeating the light pattern will make a change in overall style feel less obvious, but offer an opportunity to begin to transition toward a different long-term window plan. I am not suggesting that you use a different type of window in a new addition, however, unless it is unapologetically sympathetic toward the existing architecture. I'm sorry to say, such windows are generally a special looking, unusually shaped, great big **wow factor** sort of a thing.

Choose a window style that suits the architecture.

Doors and windows with mullions look traditional.

Casements have contemporary appeal.

bowwow to wow!

Stained Colonial-style window trim, a drab slate floor, and a lackluster fireplace are common in dated development homes. The space itself is more than adequate, and the opportunity for an enticing view is evident. A few architectural enhancements perform an architectural miracle, one little bit at a time.

1. The potential for a more interesting view down the hall is capitalized on with a very simple fireplace enhancement. Salvaged doors will create an expensive- and custom-looking raised-panel design that adds strength, importance, and architectural height to the too-wide and too-short existing stone fireplace.

2. Painting the "panels" blurs their original vertical use as doors and adds life to the stone from the resulting contrast.

3. Wood floors tie the spaces together. Perhaps the easiest part of the transformation was painting the previously wood-stained window and door trim in a color that matches the wall, eliminating the annoying visual interruption. The hall appears wider and longer in a seamless receding color scheme that encourages the eye to look through to the more exciting space ahead.

4. The oak stair is treated to a refreshing coat of high-quality paint, and the boring stock newel post is beefed up with a recessed-panel design, rendering the post substantial enough to receive an unusual copper finial. The texture and color of the aged copper add yet another layer of visual interest to the transforming view down the hall.

5. The final touch of monochromatic furnishings repeated in the sepia-tone charcoal drawing above the new mantel beckons a visit to the strong and delightful bit of architectural presence.

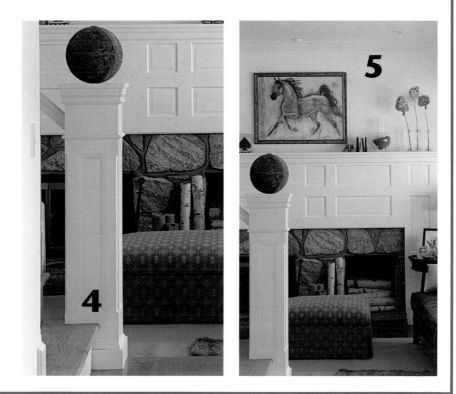

don't be a dummy

You may be eager for change, but make sure you know what you're doing.

Some time ago, in between the era of Archie and Edith Bunker and political correctness, I was called upon for my first supporting role in a **minor renovation.** My mother produced her version of a reciprocating saw and a 16-pound sledgehammer, and proceeded **to remove a wall** between the dining and living rooms, which was "getting on her nerves." She did it with the endurance of 10 men. My role was to carry out the debris and hold the ladder while my mother made repairs to the ceiling.

I think I did agree that the new burnt-orange sculptured carpet looked beautiful, and helped to choose the butter-yellow wall color that complemented the flocked wallpaper nicely. The fresh furniture arrangement included the unprecedented removal of thick plastic slipcovers, which had kept the pieces like new for as far back as I could remember. All in all, I believe she pulled it off well.

About a month later, the neighborhood building contractor was invited to the house for coffee and some fresh-from-the-oven sourdough danish. The imposing man with the giant hands sat quietly in the newly enlarged dining room. He listened to my mother's lament: no, not really, she did not exactly know what a bearing wall was but, yes, **the sag was getting worse,** and surely there was something that could be done about it.

While I can't confirm the exact conversation that followed, I can recall that my mother and father had an enduring exchange that went something like, "You don't know what you think you know about what I know," to which my father would immediately respond, "You knew enough to know better."

Anyway, the man with the big hands corrected the structurally inferior results, and my mother stuck to perfecting her danish recipe—at least for a short time.

Now what?

I share this story because while we all set out to victoriously reach a design objective, knowing what we don't know is a caveat worth examination.

Turn the page and you'll find a list that contains a few mistakes to avoid, and a few more things you might want to be very sure to know.

time out

1. Any reputable builder will offer advice and help when assessing the merits of a renovation. Even if you choose to tackle the work yourself, pay for the opinion of a qualified design professional before you get out the sledgehammer.

2. Before removing any walls, even temporarily, consult a professional and check your local building codes. Even small walls, which may not appear structural, should be assessed by a pro before they are removed.

3. Similar to any deep digging outside, if you're confident about a plan to remove walls, be sure to identify and locate electric, plumbing, and whatever else may be inside them.

4. Replacing windows with doors, doors with bigger doors, or walls with new windows requires the installation of a header. Do your homework when rearranging anything structural.

5. Think it all through, and put it on paper. Where is the heat, the water pipes, the gas lines, the electrical panel? Get to know your house, and keep accurate notes of its foibles. Keep track of important measurements, unusual locations, and so forth.

6. Sometimes even the best plans go awry; prepare for calamities, and take the time to avert dangerous situations. Shut off the water; turn off the gas; and flip the circuit breaker. Leave the "working hot" to the pros, whose brains seem to thrive on a jolt of electricity every now and then. (Only kidding!)

7. Try to have everything you need for the project on hand and a place to store everything else. Even small projects can take over the house in no time at all. Prepare to be a little overwhelmed and in a mess of some kind, and things will go more smoothly in the end.

Part 3

SAVVY DESIGN ELEMENTS

- *Materials That Matter*   **172**
- *Good Lighting*   **210**
- *Personal Color*   **226**
- *Furnishings for Comfort*   **244**
- *Collections and Displays*   **260**
- *Exclamation Points*   **280**

materials that matter

Forget the rules! Mix it up when you're choosing materials.

Modern design trends are all about **mixing** and **matching** materials. Gone is the edict that you have to use the same type of wood flooring in every room in the house, or that all of the door hardware has to match. Today, copper sinks with brushed-nickel faucets sit atop kitchen islands with countertops that are made from a different material than those in the rest of the room. Wood turns up everywhere, even in formerly off-limits applications, such as the bathroom. Environmentally sustainable products have stormed the marketplace with wildly impressive materials. A mix-and-match **trend** may simply be the reaction to having too many choices. But when you explore some outstanding examples, you'll see that mixing materials can actually result in something beautiful.

*Wood and stone are a
handsome pair.*

Mixing wood and **metal,** while not necessarily a new idea, can now be executed in bold fashion, thanks in part to the explosion of a new favorite, stainless steel. Solid maple looks handsome when you pair it with this indestructible surface, as do more traditional medium-tone woods. **Adding stone** to this mix creates a reliable counterpoint to the purity of the wood and the sleekness of the metal. The metal can be represented in appliance choices, cabinet hardware, backsplashes, sinks, and small accessories. Stone can make a big statement when you use it anywhere other than the floor.

Metal, stone, and wood add various colors and textures to a design.

For a more classic setting, painted cabinets can share a harmonious alliance with sleek stainless steel without losing their familiar or nostalgic flavor when a similarly classic tile is added to the room.

Both contemporary and traditional rooms mix sleek and warm materials.

Beyond the kitchen, equally **unlikely alliances** are being formed for fireplace surrounds, wall surfaces, and countertop material. In the bath, copper soaking tubs, wood floors, and mixed furnishings add a charm and familiar feeling and timeless strength when supported by the old stand-by, stone. Having made a complete departure from mere industrial applications, our new best friend, stainless steel, is making its way out of the kitchen and onto surfaces, such as fireplace surrounds and hardware that were once the domain of more time-honored materials.

A refurbished fireplace surround adds a modern note to this room.

Wood and upholstered furnishings reverse the cold look of white ceramic tile and stone.

can't-fail doors

Nothing says "I'm home" like the perfect pitch of a beautifully mortised, well-appointed, solid-wood door closing ever so lightly against the jamb. Powerful and lovely at the same time, a good door really matters. Scrimp a little on the hardware if you must because the door itself will be worth every penny.

Solid-wood doors come in many types of wood and with a variety of panel details and finishes. The doors can be painted, stained, or clear coated to coordinate with any style home.

Wood composite doors, more commonly known as MDF, are a little more stable than solid doors, making them better suited to withstand wet conditions. These doors must be primed and painted.

Reclaimed doors that you can find at salvage yards can add character to a house and may be the answer for a period renovation.

Singing More Praises for Wood

In the hands of a fine craftsman, choice materials will make your home rich with pattern and texture. Any detail articulated in a wonderful wood will please all of your senses at once. Window trim, wall surfaces, flooring, ceilings, and cabinetry all offer opportunities when you're searching for a way to live with fine wood. **Antique dimensional timbers** make a gutsy statement and may be used to suggest structural integrity. You can also use them in a relatively modest fashion in the form of applied beams and door casings.

Wood paneling is a classic.

Exposed wood beams make even the largest—and tallest—room feel cozy. The look can't be beat for architectural drama.

Any wood that can be touched brings a particular delight, as the feel, or "hand," of anything that is well waxed and well worn wood is a beautiful, tactile experience. If you are lucky enough to have **an exciting staircase,** this undeniable pleasure will be familiar to you.

A stunning wooden staircase will mellow beautifully over time.

A checkered pattern created with light and dark stain enlivens a surface.

Cabinet and
tile colors
that
match
look
rich.

Wood and copper looks primitive and refined.

If you long for the beauty of wood in your home and are struggling to justify its considerable cost, take the time to familiarize yourself with **woods with more humble pedigrees.** No less interesting, and sometimes exceedingly strong and stable, dimensional rough-sawn lumber, framing lumber, poplar, and laminated products maintain the presence of a finer species and can prove exceedingly useful in your home renovation, so don't count them out!

*A simple wooden beam makes
the perfect mantel on a rustic
stone fireplace.*

What Materials Cost the Most

The considerable costs associated with all the fabulous materials in the marketplace are nearly doubled when installation is factored into the budget. In fact, you may wind up paying more than the price of the material alone.

Granite must be installed by a professional.

Talking Points

"Quality is always essential whatever the price."

Billy Baldwin

For countertops and backsplashes, **lava stone, marble, granite,** or pretty much anything sold as a slab will require an on-site template to be made prior to cutting the stone, and is therefore a professional-only installation.

*Granite comes in numerous colors.
Some types have a busy pattern, while
others are solid or subtle.*

Natural stone, mesh-backed stone tile, glass tile, and **mosaics** will be very tricky to install and usually require a pro. Glass tile is probably the most deceptive in this list, so beware—there are many mistakes to be made with this seemingly modest material.

The key to installing many of these products is a suitable substrate, proper adhesive, and excellent cutting skills. Factor in the costs for mistakes when you're contemplating these products as a do-it-yourself endeavor. You might consider smaller applications as a cost-cutting compromise. Remember, if you're a novice, stay away from the glass, and please, oh please, don't try out your new tile-cutting skills on a shower-floor installation.

A sink that is mounted under a stone counter requires a special adhesive.

Glass mosaic tile can be tricky to install.

Mosaic borders can be intricate.

Mid-Price Choices

Budget-wise, **wood floors** can be a middle-of-the-road project, depending on the type of wood you choose. There is a vast difference between what antique wide-plank pumpkin pine costs versus stock 3-inch unfinished oak. Shop hard, and don't rule out engineered-wood products. These floors are highly stable— a big plus in cold climates—have superior factory finishes, and are often considered a "green" product. Manufacturers offer detailed installation instructions, and most suppliers will also provide help. Whatever type you choose, proper preparation of the subfloor is key to the project's success.

An antique wide-plank floor may be a budget buster.

An oak floor may be more affordable.

Inlaid borders will raise the price.

Keep it simple to hold down costs.

Refinishing an existing wood floor is worth the effort.

For the Budget-Minded

Maybe wood isn't your thing, and maybe you're done with maintaining a precious white marble sink. Perhaps the luscious imported limestone you covet will eat up much too much of your renovation project. Sound familiar? Could it be there is a material with a relatively reasonable price point and possibly suited for a do-it-yourself installation? Absolutely.

Ceramic, porcelain, slate, and **granite tile** counters and floors are considered manageable for do-it-yourselfers. But I must caution you that porce-lain tile is thick and difficult to cut. Products with relatively modest price points that I think are worth considering for counter surfaces include **quartzite, some solid-surfacing material, plastic laminate, concrete,** and **recycled glass.** However, these materials require professional installation. Interesting edge details will add pizzazz to these surfaces. Architects seem to especially favor solid surfacing for countertops. It takes on a whole new presence when it's cut with a wide (3-inch) edge.

Recycled glass looks modern.

Plastic laminate is most affordable.

Concrete is versatile and trendy.

Some ceramic tiles can imitate more-expensive stone.

Soapstone is practical and durable.

*Quartzite
offers many color
choices.*

Vinyl tiles can look like ceramic or stone versions.

Finally, there are a few very modestly priced materials that look perfectly stunning when properly installed. More importantly, each of these products feels great **underfoot,** rendering them a prudent choice for the kitchen, laundry room, or anywhere you spend a lot of time standing. Comfort is so often secondary to appearance, but consider the practicality of these products before you make a decision on miles of cold hard stone.

Cork, sheet vinyl, vinyl tile, and **linoleum** are durable, stable, and easy to maintain. Imaginative installations can produce even more compelling results that will last forever.

You can easily create a unique floor design with vinyl.

Talking Points

"To be successful, a room must contain the element of contrast—in forms as well as in colors and textures."

Michael Taylor

It's a practical choice for a kid's room.

My new personal favorite, which I have saved for the last but definitely not least category, are the **laminates.** Revolutionary is how I would describe these products, and I must give these manufacturers their due. Laminates are unbelievably easy to clean and maintain, very nicely priced, and incredibly durable. So beautiful when they are installed, these wonderful, environmentally sound products have a value that cannot be overstated. Try a convincing better-quality "wood" laminate, and I promise you will no longer need scatter rugs.

A wood-floor lookalike, laminate is less expensive and maintenance free.

This light-color laminate keeps this beach house guest room looking bright and airy.

An area rug can protect a floor's finish while adding pattern and color.

If you want to dress up an old floor, just paint it.

good lighting

Lighting can change the mood or function of a room.

For the moment, imagine that your makeover room is completely empty. A floor plan exists, you've selected colors, the walls are ready to paint, and the furniture is on order. Can you sense the mood in the morning, and note how the light passes through the windows as the day progresses? Is the sunlight predominantly clean, clear, early-morning light, or is it an amber afternoon glow from the west? Will a snowy winter cover reflect off the ceiling, or is there a canopy of trees outside creating a feeling of cool atmospheric calm?

My, my! What a beautiful empty room you have!

Early morning sunlight is cheerful.

Afternoon light is warm.

Northern light is cool.

The quality of the **available light** in your hypothetical empty room or any given space is the single biggest influence on the energy that exists there. Bright, sunny rooms influence and generally improve your mood, while darker, less-direct northern light feels quiet and subdued. The latter is perfect in a room for napping, watching TV, artistic pursuits, and even convalescing.

Whether as a **supplement** to the existing lighting conditions or as an enhancement to the overall design scheme, a good-quality lighting plan will enhance the **atmosphere** of any room, even those that receive more than a fair share of clean, clear sunshine.

Paneling makes the room darker and cozier.

As a design professional specializing in color and space planning, I am often asked to suggest a solution to the age-old question, "What colors will make a small or dark room seem bigger and brighter?" Now, I must admit that **I love a dark room,** and believe it's a luxury and a delight to have one in a home. A dark room has a sense of mystery and seclusion, and can become a truly delightful place, adding charm and character to a home. It is a place for quiet talks or a retreat where you can be alone with your thoughts. A tiny but interesting window nook, an unusually low ceiling, or best of all, a small corner or cranny, are some of the things that often make these places special and distinct. I love these rooms, and while I offer my **brightening strategies,** a more accurate (though possibly smug) answer to the question would be, "This is really a lighting issue."

Light is necessary to activate color, and color and brightness are a response to the lighting conditions in a room. This is not an easy concept to get your head around, but think of it this way: if it were the other way around, rooms without windows and no daylight source would still appear drab and dark no matter how well orchestrated the **lighting plan.** So to finally answer the question of how to make a small dark room seem bigger and brighter, the simple noncolor related answer is: layer the light.

Multiple light sources let you layer the lighting.

Interior lighting brightens a bank of storage cabinets.

Providing **multiple lighting sources** and controlling brightness with suitable wattages, bulb types, and dimmer switches is job one. Let the room dictate the number and style of each layer or **grouping,** depending on your finished design objective and the purpose of the room. For very large spaces and those requiring a good deal of task lighting, such as a kitchen, try to keep some of the light sources **concealed.** This tactic not only creates a dramatic effect but is a clever way to reduce glare and keep lots of light from straining your eyes.

Bouncing light on, over, and across various materials, surfaces, walls, and ceilings is the second order of business. To really brighten a space, use bright colors, lots of light-catching **reflective** surfaces, transparent furnishings, such as glass or acrylic, and framed pieces. Add a little dose of shine in the form of mirrors or metals with a dash of something glittery for good measure. These design elements will reflect and scatter the light, and more specifically, help the light to move around the room and reduce the shadows, making the space seem brighter. The addition of carefully placed **lamps for close-up tasks** completes the well-lit picture.

White walls and lots of glass reflect light.

Lighting can make an architectural statement.

For those romantic, imaginative, dark-room enthusiasts eagerly awaiting lighting-design direction, there exists an inordinate number of possibilities. Peacefully under-lit spaces use **light as art** more than illumination—an architecturally unusual conversation piece or that crazy-looking little lamp Aunt Julia gave you for your first wedding anniversary. Lacking the invigorating influence of daylight, these rooms are by definition understated, often a little quirky, and usually small in size. While a bold lighting statement might seem contradictory for a tiny room, more often than not the result is magical. Along with a dedicated task-specific light, **candlelight** is a great addition to these contemplative spaces, too. A fireplace is compelling anywhere, but spending time in a cozy room lit by a fire and candles is pretty amazing.

Ambient light, or more specifically **overall light,** is commonly placed in the center of a room, either flush or semi-flush to the ceiling. A common mistake is to make this light source too bright. Experiment with different bulbs, and try to find the lowest wattage necessary to light the room well and fill in the shadows created by any additional sources of light in the space. A general rule is to use two overhead sources. This may seem to contradict keeping ambient light to the minimum required, but remember, the objective is a well-lit space that doesn't overwhelm the eye with undue glare or brightness coming from any one overhead lamp. So while **two ambient light sources** may prove to be a luxury for a small space, a pair of them seems the ideal for most other rooms.

Good overall light should be soothing.

The right fixture adds style and light to a hallway.

You can provide overall light for hallways, foyers, and other **transitional spaces** in the same fashion. Again, consider the level of light needed in this type of space—certainly not as much as in the kitchen. Keep the overhead wattage very low; then try one or two additional sources of light, equally restrained and understated. This arrangement will add to the ambiance while reducing the overhead brightness and inherent glare. **Multiple low-level sources of light** will feel more natural and create a limitless number of possibilities for exciting fixture combinations. Together, a little lamp, multiple pendants, wall sconces, and chandeliers can define and light a space well, while supporting your general design direction.

The best way to fine tune the brightness of a light source is with a dimmer switch. Why not create **lighting scenarios** that set a scene or suit a specific occasion as you choose? Keep in mind that dimmers cannot be used with energy-efficient fluorescent bulbs. However, you can balance harsh, cool fluorescent light, such as under-cabinet task lights, with a lower-wattage incandescent light overhead.

Dimmers are considered a standard feature in a dining room, but use them in other places throughout the house where mood, atmosphere, and balance might be enhanced. Dimmers provide an "at your fingertips" ability to subtly—and energy efficiently—regulate light levels in a room from a single source. And while you're fiddling with **different light levels,** you may discover that an ordinary bath becomes a serene spa getaway, for example, or a bright kitchen turns from "Grand Central Station" into a late night bistro for midnight snacks.

Install dimmers everywhere—even on the hall's sconces.

can't-fail dimmers

Sliding dimmers operate with a sliding toggle. Position the toggle at the top for full brightness; slide it down to gradually lower the light. These are "single pole" units, and they cannot be used with multiswitch circuits.

Preset dimmers generally have an on-off switch and a separate dimmer function, allowing you to maintain any level of light you choose once the toggle or dial is set. This configuration is available for single and multiswitch circuits.

Deluxe preset dimmers have an on-off feature, as well as a small LED display that indicates the light level when the switch is tapped. Each tap of the switch lowers the brightness, is reflected on the tiny display, and can be left as a preset.

Use two chandeliers to balance light over a long table.

Exciting chandeliers do double duty, adding **architectural rhythm** to a space while solidifying the color scheme. Doubling up chandeliers adds light as well as design balance over very long tables.

Add color with glass pendants.

Open floor plans in spaces with high ceilings and complex architectural features can be challenging to light, even when applying the practice of layering. Apply **the wow factor** here to complement and balance these structures.

Alternatively, use **modern fixtures,** such as low-voltage ropes, track lighting, up lighting, pin-dot recessed lights, or novel-looking fixtures in these big exciting spaces where more classic choices could appear tentative.

Light the architecture.

Talking Points

"When we light a room, our objective is to get rid of gloom, to have enough light to feel happy."

Albert Hadley

Special lighting situations such as those required in a big, busy kitchen where multitasking and electrical demands can prove overwhelming are a rookie renovator's quagmire. So follow this suggestion for a can't-fail result: start the kitchen design by first laying out the lighting. While clearly an unconventional methodology, this formula focuses first on the lighting requirements and opportunities in the space. Once these are clearly defined, the big decisions and the small details will come together quickly as the award-winning kitchen, above, shows.

personal color

Get a handle on this magical decorating tool.

Color is complicated. The business of color can be one of careful examination and well-planned refinement, or gut instinct and casual restraint. There are rules to follow and rules to break, well-considered **philosophies,** easy-to-follow **trends,** and overly complex **theories.** Color conversations are often peppered with adjectives: vibrant, luminous, elegant, and sophisticated come to mind. Some colors are described as "reliable" or "winners," while others have terrible reputations, such as peach and pea green. Although striking, fuchsia often suffers immediate exclusion and is deemed too violent; aubergine is dark and dirty; poor burnt orange is, well, just plain ugly. Instinctive and personal, the enterprise of choosing color is further complicated by the fact that no two people see any one color in the same way. Personal preferences can spark heated debates when the delicious periwinkle you so admire is dismissed by the family in favor of Dallas Cowboy blue.

When it comes to color, should you follow your heart or the latest fashions?

So, Where Do You Begin?

While wall color is obviously the quick and arguably least-expensive means to a colorful room, just about anything in the space provides another color opportunity. Thoughtful exploration of color goes far beyond the limits of a painted perimeter or surface, no matter how beautiful. To make more meaningful color decisions, leave aside everything you know about it for the time being and focus instead on the **psychology of color.**

Do you love pink? Hate brown? Does purple make you smile? Does blue make you feel relaxed? A visceral, nearly instinctive, like or dislike of certain colors is pretty much universal. That is to say, you have a preapproved color preference, so to speak, that is generally not easily influenced. Your **personal palette** is even less rarely subject to change. Therefore, identifying these personal color preferences is the place to start.

There are many ways to add color to a room.

for a can't-fail color palette:

1. Take a trip to the paint-chip display at a home-improvement center, bringing two little brown bags. Don't panic; this is meant to be a **color experience;** you're not buying paint. Begin tossing the colors you love into one bag. Try not to give this activity too much thought. Just keep pulling colors to which you are instinctively drawn. Put in multitone chips, dark chips, bright chips; then close up the bag.

2. Now pick out chips from the colors you find objectionable, putting them into the second bag. Remember, do not think, just pick.

3. Next grab the largest black chip you can find, and you are done.

4. When you get home, find a well-lit (daylight) area to spread out the chips on a white board. Use a scissor to cut up the chips and remove the few colors that you sense may not belong. Move them around; look at them separately and in various combinations. Then notice how each color is **influenced by the combinations.** Find your colors and tape them onto the white board.

5. Working one at a time, look at how the colors from your "don't like" bag influence your finished palette. Does the brown help? Is the pink actually somewhat pretty? Still hate the purple? Does the drab olive bring back a bad memory? Out they go.

6. Your personal palette is now ready for refinement!

Art may provide color inspiration.

One tried-and-true color philosophy suggests varying the shades of a single color for a pleasing **monochromatic scheme,** which may be reflected in your personal palette. These well-balanced, serene spaces are still punctuated with some pleasing colors, especially when wider ranges of a hue are used. When using any single color, especially white, vary the materials for more impact.

An all-neutral scheme is elegant.

One strong color makes
this space soar.

If your palette has a few well-defined color combinations, then classify the **character of a color** into familiar thematic categories. Such palettes are easier to limit because interest is only partially coming from the wall color. Accessories, fabrics, and draperies each build the palette, even if the walls are neutral.

Classic

Masculine

Masculine

Feminine

Feminine

White trim pops against the strong wall color.

Some people have met only a few colors they don't like—and I'm one of them. Saturated greens, near violent magentas, and even drab olive make their way into the world of color, sometimes in larger amounts than you may desire. These are known in the trade as **"demanding colors,"** the sort you can tire of quickly, before the near heart-pounding thrill of them is gone.

If you have discovered your personal palette is exceedingly bold, use it carefully, especially if you are choosing color for the walls. **Bold wall colors** must have a good relationship with neighboring rooms and must be supported by **strong architectural features.** For this reason, the strongest colors will work beautifully in kitchens or on small wall surfaces when they are punctuated by details.

Talking Points

"Every home needs a touch of basic black...black is as exciting and attractive as any rainbow hue."

Carleton Varney

*Consider adjoining spaces when
you're choosing a wall color.*

If there is a disconnect between adjoining rooms and a strong color commitment will appear jarring, use more spirited colors for the important pieces in the room or on **featured surfaces.** Clearly, this strategy is not for the faint of heart—big colors are big commitments. But if you need a little marigold in your life, go for it!

Are you brave enough to go bold?

Bring in color with accessories.

Safe but equally individual and lively, vividly colored chairs, draperies, accessories, and textiles will make a room come alive. These **small gestures** will create a more carefree personalized feeling in a room no matter how restrained. Best of all, they can be easily changed, repurposed, or added to over time. This is a good way to mediate color disputes in the household.

Cobalt light fixtures accent this neutral kitchen with strong color.

furnishings for comfort

Furniture has to serve your practical needs and your style inclinations.

From time to time, everyone sets a goal that may be entirely unattainable. Furnishing an entire house or even one room all at once is a good example. If you tend to be an overly ambitious micro-manager, consider this: there is a continent of difference between a perfect room and a perfect piece of furniture. If you find yourself with a lot you need to get done, brave any mistakes, make necessary compromises, and enjoy the happy accidents. Be mindful that the ingredients of a beautiful room are always an **amalgamation.** Be as decisive as you can muster when you're selecting furnishings, and look at something that doesn't work as a decorating starting point—somewhere else in the house!

Create an arrangement that takes advantage of your room's best features.

Because They Said So

Many rules for furniture placement are deeply ingrained in our collective consciousness. The sofa goes on the long wall, preferably facing the focal point, with the coffee table placed about 18 inches in front of it. Then you must include two comfortable chairs with side tables and lamps, find a big spot for the television— and you're done. I know that these established **"rules" are practical,** but from time to time, a room will fight this orderly approach every inch of the way. Some of this is a product of prepackaged floor-plan formulas or the more challenging demands of an old house. A personal inventory of too big or too small, too tall or too short, weird windows and unusual ceiling heights will all add to the dilemma. The most daring people may relish an opportunity to **break a rule** now and then. If the sofa police show up to question your unconventional arrangement, I suggest you inquire about the location of the stone whereupon this law is carved.

A symmetrical arrangement looks formal.

Rooms that are not rectilinear can be challenging to arrange.

Talking Points

"Combine everything suitable that gives a room the feeling of freshness, originality, and a more beautiful atmosphere for living."

Robert Kime—Robert Kime, Ltd.

The back of the sofa creates interesting angles with the windows in this modern living room.

In Front of the Window?

Because a sofa is generally the largest horizontal furniture element in a living room, great room, or media room, it becomes **a horizontal line** in the space. Fancier designers call this a "datum." I call it a horizon. Nomenclature aside, this is more than an imaginary plane; the line will create a visual break within the space. It will also serve as the definitive point of reference by which your brain unconsciously calculates the volume, mass, scale, and proportion of the room. It is very important. This point of reference must be perfectly proportioned, or the room will feel too high, too boxy, and too long. You get the idea. This is why a sofa that is located in front of windows can be disconcerting.

But if you still want your sofa in front of a window, you can **make it work.** Keep the height of the back of the sofa, which will create the horizon in the room, in good proportion with the windows and the rest of the room.

In a traditional room, the sofa's long horizontal lines work well with the vertical lines of the windows.

The sofa police are known to wander and object with fervor to placing beds and other furnishings in front of windows, as well. If you are lucky enough to have a room with lots of windows, create the safety and security a solid wall would provide with luscious fabrics. They can form an inviting oasis where a bed can appear to float. If the room proportions or some other proportional idiosyncrasies exist, draperies can help to camouflage them. Exquisitely tailored draperies move far beyond mere dramatic flair when balance and proportion are providing the real starring role, serving the many masters of fine design: **texture, quality, elegance, sophistication, mystery,** and our dearest of friends, **delight.**

Fabric can create the feeling of a
wall behind a piece of furniture.

Another third of the room should be about form—in other words, appearance. If your sofa is dramatic and comfortable, it can count for satisfying both form and function. One single piece, and it does not matter how big or small, should be the best quality you can afford. Beware that you do not gild the lily, and be sure not to cover a lot of hard-working hand-me-down furnishings in $125-a-yard silk. Just do it with one piece. This is more device than formula.

The remaining third should be for everything else. Now you will of course be using your savvy, mixing and matching the fine and the handmade, good woods and painted pieces, exquisite and even strange. About the strange: even if everything you own comes from one store, or the entire room is looking perfectly balanced, inviting, smart, and just pretty darn swell, put something in the room that will prompt your mother to ask, "What's that doing in here?" It needs to be a contradiction or an anomaly of some sort; a pillow, a color, a vase full of tree branches, something very ugly, something unusually beautiful, a mirror, a piece of art. In other words, it should be something you appreciate because it lends a little mystery to the room.

Mix, Stir, Toss

No matter how you live, how well you decorate, and how effortlessly your rooms are coming together, let there be a final toss. **Editing** and **restraint** play an important role in a perfect room. If the essential elements are mingling nicely, your furnishings are looking and feeling ever so marvelous, and all in all you are pleased with your result, experience tells me there is something in the room that's just a little too much. Minimalist tastes, when following the rule of thirds, end up with rooms that don't quite fulfill the final portion. But devoted collectors and accumulators of all stripes are always a little over on the last third—too many pillows, too many exclamation points, too many small displays, a slew of decorations, something out of scale, something out of balance. It's in there, I know it, and it really does need to go. Invite your mother over; she'll find it.

Know when enough is enough.

A low-key
grouping of prints
fits perfectly over
this skirted table.

Nap Anyone?

Your puzzle-solving skills, willingness to experiment, make a mistake, and pull a room together like a can't-fail pro must be making you tired by now. So let's spend some time in the bedroom. Your bed, and by that I mean the box spring and mattress, should be the very best, most comfortable, delightful place to end your day that you can afford. Also, every bed should have at least a headboard, if not a distinctive frame. The bedroom is one place where a focal point is less relevant, because it is the bed that serves this function beautifully, and **the headboard creates the datum.**

I have put my foot in my mouth a number of times on the subject of headboards, the lack of which is a real pet peeve of mine. While I'll leave it to you, it really doesn't need to be much, just something to somehow designate the bed and clearly define that all important horizon line. **Beds without a headboard appear trite,** and the rooms feel inhospitable and thrown together, no matter how many pillows you have. Speaking of which, a well-tailored, minimally outfitted bed is a practicality that the design community has littered with 8 million throw pillows. This policy needs an amendment. To have to unmake the bed before retiring for the night gets tedious when there is no staff to leave chocolates behind. And because making the bed helps promote order and a general feeling of well being, it's a habit worth cultivating.

Keep throw pillows to a minimum.

collections and displays

Personalize your home with the random items that make you smile.

This will sound blunt, but I must say that anything you keep, store, obsessively hold onto, and cannot use in some meaningful way is nothing more than junk. A penchant for metal wheels, old doors, derelict window sashes, paint-can lids, baling twine, doorknobs, old brass, good silver, books, white pitchers, every doodle the kids ever painted, and oh, the glass. These are a few of the predilections of a compulsive collector. Take heart, my fellow junkers, thoughtful and well-balanced combinations of such accumulations can effectively create **rhythm** and **order** when they are displayed in an appealing and well-disciplined manner. Keeping a home well edited, but equally exhilarating in feeling, results when the **texture** and **shapes** of ordinary treasures are displayed in exciting arrangements. So-called junk, displayed proudly and deliberately in unexpected ways, becomes a glimpse into the very heart and soul of a collector. It sparks conversation and thought among you and your guests, while creating an unmistakable sense of comfort and ease in a spirited home that has a soul, as well.

Your collections say a lot about you.

Instant Memories

Like your first taste of a fine wine or the song that was playing at your first freshman dance, wonderful memories stick like glue to our inner psyches. If you are an ardent collector, you most certainly can recollect where you found your best piece of pink depression glass, when you spotted the mate to your happy little penguin salt shaker, or how elated you were to find all those antique coke bottles the previous homeowners left behind in the basement. Such feelings are **why** people collect; **what** they collect is another matter all together. Collecting anything that ignites a spark from the past with **sentiment** or **nostalgia** will rekindle your memories of where, when, and most importantly, who. Don't overlook your chances to keep those good memories as near and dear as the sugar bowl.

Talking Points

"Each item in a collection has its own story, its own memory—the search, the day you bought it, who you were with, the vacation, etcetera; a collection provides a special satisfaction and sense of achievement."

Tricia Guild

*Gold frames,
mostly of mirrors,
make a handsome
display against a
dark background.*

A tabletop grouping of shimmering glass and metal items can't fail to grab attention.

Where'd You Find All Those?

Provenance and value do not get a seat at the table of collecting madness because some of the most inspired collections cost very little. Sand from different beaches, matchbooks, hotel stationary, soil from your travels to **faraway places** kept in plain glass containers—just about anything that will enable you and your family to track your life's journey may make up your treasured collection. Furniture lacks the power to provoke emotion and thought, and besides, your distant relative is unlikely to be willing to ship tables and chairs to you from Europe. This is why "smalls," as the **antique dealers** term all those colorful, tactile, and familiar tiny objects, can become an obsession worth a little love. Choose your favorites and you will catch your friends cheerfully running their hands through the pile, sorting and stacking while chatting away, revisiting and pointing out their favorite this or that every now and then.

Frame art or make something ordinary a work of art by framing it.

Frame It

Anything in a frame becomes an **instant work of art.** Children's finger painting, calendars, recipes, the rules for a Scrabble game, all become so much more important when they are behind a little piece of glass. This practice is becoming more common thanks in part to simple, inexpensive, easy-to-assemble frames, and it is a satisfying little hobby, indeed.

I like to frame the sort of stuff that might otherwise reside in the junk drawer or, worse still, in a box in the attic. This practice keeps things organized, because business cards from potential cleaning services, maps to rarely visited cities, menus from a favorite delivery restaurant, important instructional information for stain removal, and pages cut from a catalog for those rare tulip bulbs all wind up nicely framed and on display.

Hinged shadowbox frames with soft backs to hold push pins or straight pins are terrific for this madness, and they help to keep things easily accessible by virtue of the swinging door arrangement. It's a nice solution for indecisive note keepers, coupon clippers, recipe savers, and the address-book challenged.

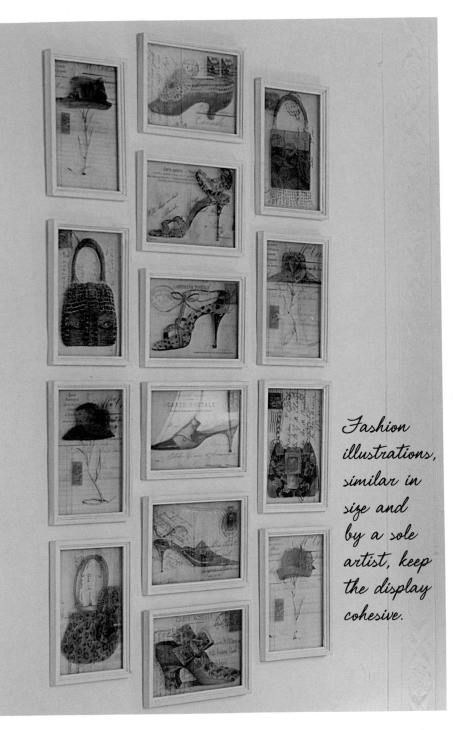

Fashion illustrations, similar in size and by a sole artist, keep the display cohesive.

*Simple line drawings balance a
tall wall without disturbing the
quiet, uncluttered environment.*

Use It

An austere, **well-edited** environment is not necessarily anathema to collectors. Admittedly, collecting can easily get away from even hyper-vigilant, super well-organized homemakers, and yes, who exactly is supposed to be doing all this dusting anyway? If you are living on a tight schedule, in a busy home, or a home full of children, a few pets, and a turtle named Moe, perhaps all this charm and nostalgia just isn't your thing.

On the other hand, a collection that **reveals** a little something about those who live in the house does not necessarily need to be heartfelt or sentimental. Utili-tarian collections offer a sense of order, character, and charisma and make for dramatic pared-down spaces. Soaps, clothespins, sponges, and everyday essentials thoughtfully displayed suggest an **organic** element and ease of style that is more suitable to simpler aesthetics. Anything that is in constant use cannot collect dust or be considered clutter, which is certainly the bane of many collectors. Serviceable items, such as pots and pans, pretty serving spoons, and lovely dishes are a great design asset in the kitchen and perform the welcoming task of a display without the burden of constant tidying.

Vintage pottery is colorful and useful.

Various sponges look artful on display.

Kid Stuff

Young children are instinctive, sometimes relentless, collectors, and managing their valued ephemera can be cumbersome. Bulletin boards make fast work of growing stacks of paper. Some structural fiberboard, a soundproofing product, is an excellent **bulletin-board** material. Available in 4 x 8-foot sheets at most home centers, it is easy to cut to any size and can be covered with any fabric, which you can affix to the underside of the board with a stapler. Cotton and muslin, even an itinerant bed sheet, will look good and function nicely, provided the fabric is thin so you can use push pins to tack up stuff. Your busy artists and young scholars can hang their latest accomplishments themselves in a special place reserved for them alone. This will instill an extra dose of pride not generally associated with displays on the refrigerator, which are often cluttered with papers and information.

Chalkboards are handy for taking messages, provide an easy-to-see and updated calendar, and can serve as an artful place for a few important phone numbers. Babysitters, young children, and anyone in a panic will greatly appreciate this precision approach to telephone-number management.

If it's neat, kids' stuff can add color and a lively look to a room.

Edit the toys from
time to time to hold
down clutter.

Three or more of anything is a collection.

Never Enough

Repurposing **garage-sale** and **thrift-shop** finds won't look tired or predictable if a little artful spin is added to the mix. Keep in mind that bold departures from a conventional formula can yield extraordinary results. Try adding two or three more items to an already overzealous display. Suddenly, it's an **instant wow;** now you've really got something powerful. This is a great technique for the constantly growing collection, so keep it going until there isn't another inch, but delete less-prized pieces when a new one arrives.

Stick to one
color, or repeat
shapes.

exclamation points

Add a finishing touch to your room with a focal point or two.

Wow. That's the word I used first when I began pulling together this chapter. Pictures of fireplaces, bookcases, and important art pieces started filling a box, thanks to Mark, my devoted husband and accomplice in this endeavor. Things started to get a little sticky, however, when I began to ask for items such as clocks, glorious windows, peculiar furnishings, and all things gigantic. My cohort was dubious, so I crossed out the word "wow" and wrote **"focal points"** on the box. All was right with the world, and we went along pretty well thereafter, until the final straw: a birdcage.

"How in the world can a birdcage be considered a focal point?" he asked.

I hope by now that sharing my point of view, which is often labeled "eccentric," has opened your eyes to new ways to see and perceive great design. My own good fortune to work with accomplished builders, artisans, and craftspersons of every ilk, photographers, interior designers, architects, and visionaries is a humbling and awe-inspiring way to live a life. I have been flattered to share my experience with you here. And so I trust you will agree with me that a wonderful birdcage that adds life, rhythm, and **pulse** to a room is a focal point, or an "exclamation point," as I like to say, indeed.

Talking Points

"Strategically incorporating art and eclectic accessories enhances a room's unique features and creates a natural sense of scale and timelessness."

Keith Baltimore—Baltimore Design Group

I rest my case!

The Fire Within

A fireplace says "home" like no other feature in a house. In fact, home and hearth remain an **enduring** traditional expression of a life well lived. The element of fire evokes mystery and passion, which is a nice combination in the bedroom, and adds a landmark and gathering spot to any room, despite a lack of necessity. The **lure of a fire provokes** all sorts of emotions, and I am remaining neutral as to whether a roaring wood-burning classic is superior to the new-fangled gas-burning units. Gas inserts grow more diminutive every day, and finishing them with all sorts of tempting materials adds to their attraction.

Match your style with finishing details that reflect either a casual or formal look.

A sleek stone surround suits the look of this modern room.

Fire is fire, and while there are safety issues, a working fireplace in the house will raise the **delight quotient,** to be sure. If you are unable to add a fireplace or you have one that is out of order, out-fit the room with a special mantel and include all of the accoutrements generally surrounding a working unit. To overcome the lack of a firebox and fire, let your imagination run wild with candles, wood collections, lovely florals, and the like. This never looks as crazy as it sounds, and you'll be thrilled to pieces when the holidays roll around.

Nothing beats a fireplace for ambiance.

Built-in bookcases flanking a fireplace create the ultimate focal point.

A Fine Library

A fine library—does it get any better than that? Reading, either by necessity, habit, or desire transcends hobby or interest. It's not exactly a sport, and not quite a creative outlet either. The adjectives that can be attached to reading are many: purposeful, inspiring, stimulating, stirring, contemplative, thoughtful, restorative, educational, heartening. While I am stepping onto some thin ice here, I'd like to put forth a personal opinion and suggest that reading and **book collecting** is, in fact, an art. Skill, discipline, and technique? How else can an afternoon spent teetering in the hammock with your favorite John Irving novel in one hand and an ice-cold mojito in the other be described? And you thought I was getting all haughty and esoteric, didn't you? While books can lift their surroundings to very distinguished heights, they also provide opportunities to experience many feelings. Add a bookcase to a room if you can. Experiment with ingenious display alternatives while you are collecting. If you already own a fine library, unless the books are **valuable** first editions, stack them here and there in always-evolving, ever-growing arrangements.

Capitalize on the character books bring to a room and plan your color choices accordingly. The covers, bindings, and jackets display a lot of it. Do not make the mistake of removing the jackets in favor of a solid-color spine; that's a decorators' ploy and a book dealers' nightmare. According to my best friends, Jim and Annmarie, professional book dealers and skilled, disciplined readers, most of a book's value is in the jacket.

A wall of books delineates the reading area.

A Natural Situation

Exclamation points, which can be and often are focal points, add life and vitality to a room. If the exclamation point is an organic thing—water, earth, fire, air, plant, fish, dog, or cat, to name a few—so much the better. Living in **harmony** with nature is awfully nice, affecting your mood and, some say, your fate for the better. These tenants are a tiny slice of the study of **feng shui,** an ancient Chinese teaching that suggests improving an invisible force, termed "chi," will affect the circumstance and quality of life in the surrounding environment. For more practical purposes, these teachings seem logical and sound.

An unusual arrangement of fresh flowers is a lovely exclamation point.

The dramatic colors and shapes in
nature easily command attention.

While it may not be a sure bet that adding plants or a water feature to a room will improve the flow of your day, it is nonetheless a bet worth hedging. My feeble explanation is poor at best and warrants further reading in a nice welcoming chair. For now, add all the life you can to your home and see if it doesn't improve the mood of things.

Change the flowers with the seasons.

Look for something unusual to incorporate into your design.

What Did You Say That Is?

Don't forget to add a little dose of something **strange.** It will create conversation, spark a little interest, and if you really get this right, illustrate a side of your personality only those who know you best can appreciate. You'll know you've done well if removing the item after a while leaves the room feeling a little unfinished. I can't even begin to speculate what your particular strange item could be, but it helps if there is some sentiment attached to it, that it is not too precious, and noticing it makes you smile. Don't mistake strange with weird, though. In our hurried lives, the finer things are easily overlooked or cast aside. A well-ironed linen tablecloth or a beautifully outfitted table may appear a little strange too, I am sorry to say. Keep your **options open,** and delegate this job to someone else if you're unsure. Send the kids to find a big rock, or let your husband put the old brake shoe from his prized race car on the bookcase.

Now you are ready to embark on your own can't-fail journey. So go make some *perfect* and have fun. Off you go!

resources

The following list of manufacturers and associations is meant to be a general guide to additional industry and product-related sources. It is not intended as a listing of products and manufacturers represented by the photographs in this book.

MANUFACTURERS

Above View
414-744-7118
www.aboveview.com
Makes ornamental ceiling tiles.

All Multimedia Storage
866-603-1700
www.allmultimediastorage.com
Manufactures media storage.

Amtico International Inc.
404-267-1900
www.amtico.com
Manufactures vinyl flooring.

Architectural Products by Outwater
800-835-4400
www.outwater.com
Manufactures hardwood and plastic moldings, niches, frames, hardware, and other products.

Armstrong World Industries
717-397-0611
www.armstrong.com
Manufactures floors, cabinets, ceilings, and ceramic tiles.

Benjamin Moore & Co.
www.benjaminmoore.com
Manufactures paint.

Central Fireplace
800-248-4681
www.centralfireplace.com
Manufactures fireplaces

Congoleum Corp.
800-274-3266
www.congoleum.com
Manufactures resilient, high-pressure plastic-laminate flooring.

Corian, a div. of DuPont
800-426-7426
www.corian.com
Manufactures solid surfacing.

Crossville, Inc.
931-484-2110
www.crossvilleinc.com
Manufactures porcelain, stone, and metal tile.

Couristan, Inc.
800-223-6186
www.couristan.com
Manufactures natural and synthetic carpets and rugs.

Dex Studios
404-753-0600
www.dexstudios.com
Creates custom concrete sinks, tubs, and countertops.

Elfa
www.elfa.com
Manufactures storage products and closet
systems.

Expanko, Inc.
800-345-6202
www.expanko.com
Manufactures cork and rubber flooring.

Formica Corp.
513-786-3525
www.formica.com
Manufactures plastic laminate and solid
surfacing.

Häfele America Co.
800-423-3531
www.hafeleonline.com
Manufactures cabinet hardware.

Hartco Hardwood Floors
800-769-8528
www.hartcoflooring.com
Manufactures engineered hardwood and solid-
wood flooring.

Ikea
www.ikea.com
Manufactures furniture and home-organization
accessories.

Jian & Ling Bamboo
757-368-2060
www.jianlingbamboo.com
Manufactures vertical and horizontal cut
bamboo flooring.

Lightology
866-954-4489
www.lightology.com
Manufactures lighting fixtures.

Maytag Corp.
800-688-9900
www.maytag.com
Manufactures major appliances.

Merillat
www.merillat.com
Manufactures cabinets.

Seagull Lighting Products, Inc.
856-764-0500
www.seagulllighting.com
Manufactures lighting fixtures.

Sherwin-Williams
www.sherwinwilliams.com
Manufactures paint.

Sure-Fit, Inc.
888-754-7166
www.surefit.com
Manufactures readymade slipcovers and
pillows.

Tarkett
www.tarkett-floors.com
Manufactures vinyl, laminate, tile, and wood
flooring.

Toto USA
770-282-8686
www.totousa.com
Manufactures toilets, bidets, sinks, and
bathtubs.

ASSOCIATIONS

**National Association of the Remodeling
Industry (NARI)**
800-611-6274
www.nari.org
A professional organization for remodelers,
contractors, and design-build professionals.

**National Kitchen and Bath Association
(NKBA)**
800-652-2776
www.nkba.org
A national trade organization for kitchen and
bath design professionals. It offers consumers
product information and a referral service.

glossary

Accent Lighting A type of lighting that highlights an area or object to emphasize that aspect of a room's character.

Ambient Lighting General illumination that surrounds a room. There is no visible source of the light.

Backlighting Illumination coming from a source behind or at the side of an object.

Backsplash The vertical part at the rear and sides of a countertop that protects the adjacent wall.

Built-In Any element, such as a bookcase or cabinetry, that is built into a wall or an existing frame.

Casegoods A piece of furniture used for storage, including cabinets, dressers, and desks.

Clearance The amount of space between two fixtures, the centerlines of two fixtures, or a fixture and an obstacle, such as a wall.

Code A locally or nationally enforced mandate regarding structural design, materials, plumbing, or electrical systems that state what you can or cannot do when you build or remodel.

Color Wheel A pie-shaped diagram showing the range and relationships of pigment and dye colors.

Complementary Colors Hues directly opposite each other on the color wheel. As the strongest contrasts, complements tend to intensify each other.

Contemporary Any modern design (after 1920) that does not contain traditional elements.

Cove 1. A built-in recess in a wall or ceiling that conceals an indirect light source. 2. A concave recessed molding that is usually found where the wall meets the ceiling or floor.

Daybed A bed made up to appear as a sofa. It usually has a frame that consists of a headboard, a footboard, and a sideboard along the back.

Dimmer Switch A switch that can vary the intensity of the light it controls.

Distressed Finish A decorative paint technique in which the final paint coat is sanded and battered to produce an aged appearance.

Faux Finish A decorative paint technique that imitates a pattern found in nature.

Fittings The plumbing devices that bring water to the fixtures, such as faucets.

Focal Point The dominant element in a room or design, usually the first to catch your eye.

Ground-Fault Circuit Interrupter (GFCI) A safety circuit breaker that compares the amount of current entering a receptacle with the amount leaving. If there is a discrepancy of 0.005 volt, the GFCI breaks the circuit in a fraction of a second. GFCIs are required in damp areas of the house.

Grout A mortar that is used to fill the spaces between tiles.

Hardware Wood, plastic, or metal plated trim found on the exterior of furniture, such as knobs, handles, and decorative trim.

Harmonious Color Scheme Also called analogous, a combination focused on neighboring hues on the color wheel. The shared underlying color generally gives such schemes a coherent flow.

Hue Another term for specific points on the pure, clear range of the color wheel.

Incandescent Lighting A bulb (lamp) that converts electric power into light by passing electric current through a filament of tungsten wire.

Indirect Lighting A more subdued type of lighting that is not head-on, but rather reflected against another surface such as a ceiling.

Inlay A decoration, usually consisting of stained wood, metal, or mother-of-pearl, that is set into the surface of an object in a pattern and finished flush.

Modular Units of a standard size, such as pieces of a sofa, that can be fitted together.

Molding An architectural band used to trim a line where materials join or create a linear decoration. It is typically made of wood, plaster, or a polymer.

Occasional Piece A small piece of furniture for incidental use, such as end tables.

Orientation The placement of any object or space, such as a window, a door, or a room, and its relationship to the points on a compass.

Sectional Furniture made into separate pieces that coordinate with each other. The pieces can be arranged together as a large unit or independently.

Slipcover A fabric or plastic cover that can be draped or tailored to fit over a piece of furniture.

Task Lighting Lighting that concentrates in specific areas for tasks, such as preparing food, applying makeup, reading, or doing crafts.

Tone Degree of lightness or darkness of a color.

Track Lighting Lighting that utilizes a fixed band that supplies a current to movable light fixtures.

Trompe L'oeil Literally meaning "fool the eye;" a painted mural in which realistic images and the illusion of more space are created.

Uplight Also used to describe the lights themselves, this is actually the term for light that is directed upward toward the ceiling.

Valance Short curtain panel that hangs along the top of a window.

Vanity a bathroom floor cabinet that usually contains a sink and storage space.

Veneer High-quality wood that is cut into very thin sheets for use as a surface material.

Wainscoting A wallcovering of boards, plywood, or paneling that covers the lower section of an interior wall and usually contrasts with the wall surface above.

Work Triangle The area bounded by the lines that usually connect the sink, range, and refrigerator. A kitchen may have multiple work triangles. In an ideal triangle, the distances between appliances are from 4 to 9 feet.

index

Accessorizing, 15
Acoustics, 62
Addictive strategies, 22
Adjoining spaces, color choice and, 238–239
Ambiance, 285
Ambient lights, 29, 217
Architectural elements, 10, 50–170; color and, 236; daily needs
        in, 132–147; entries as, 50–53, 56–59; exterior
        versus interior style, 54–55; fireplaces as,
        282–285; hidden spaces and, 98–115; lighting
        and, 222, 224; in perfect room, 28, 33; perimeters
        as, 60–71; practicality and, 116–131; rhythm as,
        84, 88; staircases as, 72–81; windows as,
        148–166
Architectural salvage, 76
Area rugs, 53, 70, 208
Artwork, 33. See also Collections and displays; color inspiration
        from, 231; creating, out of the ordinary, 85;
        drawing attention to, 154; in entries, 53; framed,
        268–270; on staircase walls, 78–79

Backsplashes, materials for, 190
Balance, 33
Baldwin, Billy, 143, 188
Balk, Beverly, 45
Balusters, 74
Balustrades, 74
Bathroom: niches in, 104; organization of, 133–135
Bedroom, furnishings for, 258–259
Billinkoff, Donald, 26, 42
Black, 230, 237, 242–243
Bookcases, 28, 29, 34; built-in, 286–287; niche for, 103–104
Borders, 193, 196
Brightening strategies, 212–213
Budget, 26–35, 42
Bulletin boards, 274–275

Cabinets: built-in, 123; matching tile colors and, 185; painted,
        176
Candlelight, 216
Carpentry issues, 20
Casement windows, 162, 165
Ceiling beams, 28, 34, 182–183, 187
Ceilings, 11; color for, 12; crown moldings for, 68, 69, 70;

decorative medallions on, 68–71; height, features
        and shape of, 62; high, 63–65; importance of, 61
Ceramic tile, 179, 198, 200
Chair rails, 68
Chalkboards, 274–275
Chandeliers, 11, 13, 222
Children, collections of, 274–277
Closets: converting, into pantry, 110–111; open, 112–113;
        organization of, 132, 139–142; removing door
        from, 112–113; walk-in, 138
Clutter, 88
Coffee table, doubling of ottoman as, 32
Coleman, Cindy, 120
Collections and displays, 33, 260–279; of children, 274–277;
        display of, 83, 89–92, 261–265, 278–279;
        editing of, 15; using, 272–273
Colonial-style windows, 166
Color(s), 226–243; absence of, 45; in adjoining spaces,
        238–239; architectural elements and, 236; art
        and, 231; choosing, 12; home site and, 30;
        lighting and, 212, 213, 215, 241; paint, 30;
        personality and, 39, 228; punch, 12, 54, 80, 233,
        236; for staircases, 74, 80
Color scheme: all-neutral, 232; changing exterior, 54;
        monochromatic, 12, 167, 232; reciprocal, 54
Comfort, choosing furnishings for, 14
Command center, 128–131
Computers in command center, 129, 130
Concrete, 198, 199
Copper, wood and, 186
Cork, 202
Countertops, materials for, 177, 190
Crawl space, using space in, 104
Crown molding, for ceiling, 68, 69, 70
Curb appeal, 56

Daily needs, 132–147
Dark rooms, 212
Datum, 249, 258
Dead space, innovative ways of using, 103–104
Decorative ceiling medallions, 68–71
Delight quotient, 284
Design book: carpentry issues in, 20; doodling in, 21; goals in,
        19; labor list in, 25; making, 18; measurements

in, 19; purpose in, 22; reviewing in, 23; room feel in, 21; taking notes in, 19; wishing in, 21, 23

Design elements: architecture, 10, 50–170; collections and displays, 15, 260–279; color, 12, 226–243; exclamation points, 16, 34, 280–293; furnishings, 14, 244–259; lighting, 13, 210–225; materials, 11–12, 172–209

Details, paying attention to, 82–97

Dimmers, 220, 221

Dining room, framing view into, 155

Doors: in Federal style, 58; French, 161; front, 50–51; glass, 153; mullions for, 164; multiple, 156; painting of panels, 166; placement of, 58; pocket, 110; reclaimed, 180; removing, from closet, 112–113; salvaged, 166; solid-wood, 180; wood composite, 180

Dormer windows, 160

Double-hung windows, 162

Dressing table, 11

Drywall, absorption of sound by, 65

Dubus, Andre, 124

Engineered-wood products, 194

Entries, 50, 52–53; artwork in, 53; framing of, 155; garage as, 56; mirror wall in, 52–53; mudroom as, 56; side, 56–59; soaring, 62; staircases in, 73

Environmentally sustainable products, 172

Estimates, getting, 25

Exclamation points, 16, 34, 280–293

Exterior, relationship with interior, 54–55, 58

Falco, Patrick, 37

Feng shui, 288

Finial, adding unusual, 76

Finishing touches, adding, to rooms, 280–293

Fire codes, 74

Fireplaces, 216, 282–285

Fireplace surrounds, 177, 178

First impressions, 56, 62

Flooring: hardwood, 28; painting, 209; wood, 167, 172, 194–197

Floor plans, 37, 210, 224

Flower arrangements, 289, 291

Fluorescent lighting, 220

Focal points, 16, 280, 288

Form follows function, 37

Frame art, 268–270

French doors, 161

Function, 116

Furnishings, 244–259; arrangement of, 21, 32, 245–250;

choosing for comfort and style, 14; editing and, 256; fabric and, 250–251; proportion and, 252; rule of thirds and, 253–254, 256

Glass, 11; recycled, 198; for windows, 151

Glass doors, 153

Glass tile, 192, 193

Gold leaf, 11

Granite, 188, 190, 191, 198

Great rooms, popularity of two-story, 62

Green products, 194

Grouping of similar objects, 83–84, 89–92

Guild, Tricia, 262

Hadley, Albert, 92, 225

Halls, 159; lighting for, 218; wooden floor for, 167

Hardwood floors, 28

Headboard, need for, 258

Hidden spaces, 98–115, 143

Higgins, Jackie, 38

Hobby, finding space for, 135–136

Home, organization of, to fit needs and lifestyle, 116–131

Home-renovation projects, costs in, 26–35

Horizon, 249

Informal sketches, 47

Inlaid borders, 196

Interior, creating relationship with exterior, 54–55, 58

Inventory, 24–25, 46

Kime, Robert, 247

Kitchen: command center in, 128–131; countertops in, 172; islands in, 172; lighting for, 218, 220, 225; practicality in, 118–121; shelving in, 99; spice cabinet in wall of, 100–101

Knee wall, using space in, 104

Labor list, compiling, 25

Laminates, 198, 199, 206–207

Lamps, 13, 29, 215

Laundry room, 124–127

Lavastone, 190

Lighting, 210–225; ambient, 29, 217; chandeliers as, 11, 13, 222; color and, 212, 213, 215, 241; concealed, 214; dimmers and, 220, 221; fluorescent, 220; for kitchen, 218, 220, 225; lamps as, 13, 29, 215; mood and, 210, 211; multiple sources of, 213–214, 218; natural, 153, 210–211; overhead, 217; pendants as, 158, 218, 223; plan for, 211,

213; recessed, 224; in special situations, 225; task, 214; track, 29, 224

Linoleum, 202

Magazine clippings, looking at, 21
Marble, 190
Materials, choosing right, 1–12, 172–209
Measurements, importance of, 19
Metal, 11; mixing wood and, 174
Millwork, 10, 65
Mirrors, 11
Mirror wall, 52–53
Mistakes, avoiding, 169–170
Monochromatic color scheme, 12, 68, 70, 167, 232
Mood, lighting and, 210, 211
Moose head, 34
Morris, William, 74
Mosaics, 192, 193
Mudrooms, 56, 124
Mullions, 11, 164

Natural lighting, 153, 210
Natural stone, 192
Negative space, 104, 114–115
Newel posts, 76–77, 81
Niche: in bathroom, 104; for bookcase, 103–104; breaking up a large wall with, 108
Noise, controlling, 62
Notes, taking, on walk through, 19

Oak floors, 195
Oak stairs, 167
Objects: grouping of similar, 83, 89–91; vintage, 94–97
Ordinary, creating artwork out of the, 85
Organization: of closets, 132, 139–142; of pantry, 122–123; value of, 116–117
Ottomans, doubling of, as coffee table, 32

Paint: adding personality by combining with stain, 75; color of, 30; stripping lead, 81
Painted cabinets, 176
Pairs, grouping in, 92
Paneling, 212
Pantry, organizing, 110–111, 122–123
Paper, dreaming on, 18–23
Parish, Sister, 280
Pendants, 158, 223
Perfect rooms: before and after, 36–45; designing, 10–17
Period homes, 160

Personality, adding with color, 39
Pet, making space for, 143
Planning, 41; importance of, 46; materials in, 46
Pocket doors, 110
Porcelain, 198
Practicality in the kitchen, 118–121
Professional installation, 188, 190, 192
Proportion, 40
Punch colors, adding, 12, 54
Punch windows, 150
Purpose, adding, 22

Quantity, 135; grouping, in unusual, 84
Quartzite, 198, 201

Rafters, opening ceiling to the, 64
Recessed lights, 224
Reclaimed doors, 180
Recycled glass, 198
Reflective surfaces, 215
Repetitiveness, 88
Rhythm, 33, 84, 88
Risers, adding color to, 74
Rooms: all-white, 45; cost comparison of side-by-side, 27; creating visual, 78–79; little things in making special, 82–97; square feet in typical, 100
Rugs: area, 53, 70, 208; as counterpoint to ceiling, 68
Rule of thirds, 253–254, 256

Saladino, John, 50, 60
Salvaged doors, 166
Sardar, Zahid, 159
Scale, 40, 46, 47
Sheet vinyl, 202, 204–205
Shelves: adjustable, 107; extra, in kitchen, 99; floating, 105; in negative space, 114–115
Side entries, 56–59
Sinks, mounting under stone counters
Slate, 198
Soapstone, 200
Solid-surfacing materials, 198
Solid-wood doors, 180
Sound, absorption of, 65
Space: creating custom design from small, 106; finding, for hobby, 135–136; hidden, 98–115, 143; human response to, 60; making special, 45; need for, 60; negative, 104, 114–115; using, 119–120
Spice cabinet, 100–101
Spindles, painting, 74

Stain, adding personality by combining with paint, 75
Stainless steel, 174
Staircases, 72–81; adding personality to, 75; current trends for, 74; in entry hall, 73; finial for, 76; newel posts for, 76–77, 81; painting, 74, 80; personalizing, 74; rehabilitation of, 72, 76, 81; wooden, 167, 184
Stair railings, 74
Stone, 179; addition of, 174; pairing with wood, 173
Stone counters, sinks mounted under, 192
Stone tile, 192
Stone walls, character of, 66–67
Storage for television, 144–147
Style, choosing furnishings for, 14
Subtractive strategies, 22

Table display, fresh fruit as, 86
Task lighting, 214
Taylor, Michael, 106, 204
Teich, Marlaina, 41
Television storage, 144–147
Texture, mixing, 28
Themes, 91, 136–137
Throw pillows, 258, 259
Tiles: ceramic, 179, 198, 200; glass, 192, 193; matching cabinets and, 185; stone, 192; vinyl, 202
Time management, 35
Track lights, 29, 224
Transitional spaces, lighting for, 218

Understatement, 93
Utility rooms, 124

Vacuum, storage of, 102–103
Varney, Carleton, 237
View, framing of, with windows, 148–166
Vignettes, 53, 150, 156
Vintage homes, 160
Vintage objects, 94–97
Vinyl, sheet, 202, 204
Vinyl tile, 202
Visual rooms, creating, 78–79
Volunteers, recruiting, 25

Walk-in closet, 138
Walk through, taking notes on, 19
Wallpaper, 12
Walls: artwork on, 78–79; breaking up large, 108; extra space between, 100–101; importance of, 61; removing, 168; stone, 66–67

White room, 45, 215
Windows, 10, 148–166; casement, 162, 165; Colonial-style, 166; creating bank of, 58, 59; in defining house, 148; dormer, 160; double-hung, 162; fenestration of, 148; glass for, 151; mullions for, 11, 164; punch, 150; replacing existing, 148; sizes of, 149, 157; styles of, 148, 149
Window seats, 12, 152, 160; surrounds for, 10
Window treatments, 28, 152
Wiring, planning of, for television, 14
Wish list, honing down, 24–25
Wood: absorption of sound by, 65; copper and, 186; mixing metal with, 174; stone and, 173
Wood composite doors, 180
Wood floors, 167, 172, 194–197
Wood paneling, 181
Wow factor, 224

credits

All photos by Mark Samu

Page 1: Artistic Designs by Deidre **page 3:** Lucianna Samu Design **page 5:** Donald Billinkoff AIA **page 6:** The Michaels Group **page 8:** Donald Billinkoff AIA **pages 9–17:** *all* design: Noli Design **page 27:** *left all* design: Lucianna Samu Design; *right all* design: Steven Goldgram Design **pages 28–31:** *all* design: Lucianna Samu Design **pages 32–33:** *both* design: Steven Goldgram Design **page 34:** design: Lucianna Samu Design **pages 36–37:** *all* design: Falco Designs Inc. **pages 38–39:** *all* design: Beach Glass Designs **pages 40–41:** *all* design: Marlaina Teich Designs **pages 42–43:** *all* design: Ziering Ineriors **pages 44–45:** *all* design: Beverly Balk Interiors **page 50:** design: Peter Cook, AIA **page 51:** design: Lucianna Samu Design **page 52:** design: Carolyn Miller Design **pages 54–55:** *both* design: Ellen Roche Architect **page 57:** design: Kollath-McCann Creative Services **page 58–59:** *all* design: Lucianna Samu Design **page 61:** design: D. Reis Contracting **page 62:** design: Kitchen Design By Ken Kelly **page 63:** design: D. Reis Contracting **pages 64–65:** *both* design: Balzer Hodge Tuck AIA **page 66:** design: Ellen Roche Architect **page 67:** design: Witt Construction, Inc. **page 68–71:** *all* design: Lucianna Samu Design **page 73:** design: D. Reis Contracting **page 75:** design: Ellen Roche Architect **page 76:** design: Lucianna Samu Design **page 77:** design: Tom Frost AIA **page 78:** *both* design:Artistic Designs by Deidre **page 79:** design: Balzer Hodge Tuck AIA **page 80:** design: Donald Billinkoff AIA **page 81:** *both* design: Lucianna Samu Design **page 87:** design: Jackie Talmo Decor **page 88:** design: Eileen Katherine Boyd Interiors **page 90–91:** design: Eileen Katherine Boyd Interiors **page 93:** design: Mojo-Stumer Architect **page 95:** design: Kitchen Design By Ken Kelly **page 96–97:** design: Charles Reilly Design **page 98:** design: Peter Cook AIA **page 99:** design: Lucianna Samu Design **page 100–101:** *both* design: Jean Stoffer Design **page 102–103:** *both* design: Lucianna Samu Design **page 104:** design: Charles Reilly Design **page 105:** design: Correia Design **page 106:** design: Andreas Letkovsky Architect **pages 108–109:** design: Correia Design **page 110–111:** *both* design: Carpen House **page 112:** design: Lucianna Samu Design **page 113:** design: Paula Yednak Design **pages 114–115:** *all* design: Lucianna Samu Design **page 117:** design: Charles Reilly Design **page 118:** *left* design: Falco Designs Inc.; *right* design Doug Mayer AIA **page 119:** design: Jean Stoffer Design **page 120:** *all* design: Carpen House **page 121:** *top* design: Jean Stoffer Design; *bottom* design: Lucianna Samu Design **pages 122–125:** *all* design: Ellen Roche Architect **page 127:** design: Lucianna Samu Design **page 128:** design: SD Atelier Architect **page 129:**

all design: Eileen Katherine Boyd Interiors **pages 130–131:** *all* design: Lucianna Samu Design **page 132:** design: Ellen Roche Architect **page 133:** design: Lucianna Samu Design **page 134:** design: Courtesy Mill Neck Manor **page 135:** design: Susan Fredman Design **page 136:** design: Ellen Roche Architect **page 137:** *bottom* design: Correia Design **page 138:** design: D. Reis Contracting **page 139:** *both* design: Ellen Roche Architect **page 142:** design: Lucianna Samu Design **page 143:** *both* design: Ellen Roche Architect **page 144:** design: D. Reis Contracting **page 145:** design: Lucianna Samu Design **page 146:** *top* design: Charles Reilly Design **page 146:** *bottom* design: Lucianna Samu Design **page 147:** design: Artistic Designs by Deidre **page 148:** design: Eileen Katherine Boyd Interiors **page 149:** design: Eileen Katherine Boyd Interiors **pages 150–151:** *both* design: Jean Stoffer Design **page 152:** *top* design: Eileen Katherine Boyd Interiors; *bottom* design: Beverly Balk Interiors **page 154:** design: Ellen Roche Architect **page 156:** design: Balzer Hodge Tuck AIA **page 157:** design: Amedore Homes **page 158:** design: Donald Billinkoff AIA **page 159:** design: Falk & Gordon Design **pages 160–161:** *both* design: Lucianna Samu Design **page 163:** *top* design: Doug Moyer Architect; *bottom* design: Jean Stoffer Design **page 165:** design: Balzer Hodge Tuck AIA **page 166–167:** *all* design: Lucianna Samu Design **page 173:** design: T. Michaels Construction **page 175:** design: Witt Construction, Inc. **page 177:** design: Donald Billinkoff AIA **page 178:** design: Eileen Katherine Boyd Interiors **page 179:** *top* design: Doug Moyer Architect **page 180:** *left* design: SD Atelier Architect; *right* design: Dean Durst Construction **page 181:** *both* design: Eileen Katherine Boyd Interiors **pages 182–183:** design: Balzer Hodge Tuck AI **page 184:** *left* design: Ellen Roche Architect; *right* design: Dean Durst Construction **page 185:** design: Kitchen Design By Ken Kelly **page 186:** design: Bonacio Construction **page 187:** design: Capital Construction **page 188:** design: Jean Stoffer Design **page 189:** design: Kitchen Design By Ken Kelly **page 190:** *left* design: Kitchen Design By Ken Kelly; *right* design: Ellen Roche Architect **page 191:** design: Charles Reilly Design **page 192:** design: Artistic Designs by Deidre **page 193:** *top* design: Kitchen Design By Ken Kelly **page 194:** design: Eileen Katherine Boyd Interiors **page 195:** design: Carolyn Miller Design **page 197:** design: D. Reis Contracting **page 198:** design: Kitchen Design By Ken Kelly **page 199:** *top* design: Charles Reilly Design; *bottom* design: Andreas Letkovsky Architect **page 200:** *top* design: Mannington Tile; *bottom* design: Lucianna Samu Design **page 201:** design: Artistic Designs by Deidre **page 202:** *left* design: Lucianna Samu Design; *right* design: The Breakfast Room **page 203:** design: Charles Reilly Design **page 204:** *top* design: SD Atelier Architect;

bottom design: Charles Reilly Design **pages 205–206:** *both* design: Charles Reilly Design **pages 207–208:** design: Lucianna Samu Design **page 209:** *top* design: Doug Moyer Architect **page 210:** design: Ellen Roche Architect **page 211:** *top* design: Blairhouse Interiors; *bottom* design: Saratoga Signature Interiors **page 212:** design: Falco Designs Inc. **page 213:** design: Evergreen House Interiors **page 214:** design: Carpen House **page 215:** design: Eileen Katherine Boyd Interiors **page 216:** design: Correia Design **page 217:** design: Eileen Katherine Boyd Interiors **page 218:** design: SD Atelier Architect **page 219:** design: Falco Designs Inc. **page 220:** design: Lucianna Samu Design **page 221:** design: Lutron Lighting **page 223:** design: Carpen House **page 224:** *left* design: Donald Billinkoff AIA; *right* Brian Shore Architect **page 229:** *top* design: Eileen Katherine Boyd Interiors **page 231:** design: Eileen Katherine Boyd Interiors **page 232:** design: Steven Goldgram Design **page 235:** *bottom left* design: Eileen Katherine Boyd Interiors **page 236:** design: Steven Goldgram Design **page 237:** *top* design: Kitchen Design By Ken Kelly; *bottom* design: Kollath-McCann Creative Services **page 238:** design: Charles Reilly Design **page 239.** *top* design: Dean Durst Construction; *bottom* design: Lucianna Samu Design **page 240:** *all* design: Eileen Katherine Boyd Interiors **page 241:** design: Kitchen Design By Ken Kelly **pages 242–243:** *all* design: Sherrill Canet Design **page 244–245:** design: Ellen Roche Architect **pages 248–249:** *top* design: Mercedes Courland Design; *bottom* design: Baltimore Design Center **page 250:** design: Katherine McCoy Architect **page 251:** design: Sherrill Canet Design **page 253–255:** *all* design: KJ Interior Design **page 256–257:** *both* design: Aprile Marchesano Design **page 258:** *left* design: Witt Construction, Inc; *right* design: Donald Billinkoff AIA **pages 261–263:** *both* design: Eileen Katherine Boyd Interiors **pages 264–265:** design: Tarasoff Interiors **page 266:** design: Falco Designs Inc. **page 267:** design: Mercedes Courland Design **page 269:** design: Eileen Katherine Boyd Interiors **page 270:** design: Courtesy Mill Neck Manor **page 271:** design: Sam Scofield Architect **page 275:** design: Lee Najman Design **page 279:** design: Beverly Balk Interiors **page 282:** design: Lucianna Samu Design **page 285:** design: Eileen Katherine Boyd Interiors **page 206:** *bottom* design: Lucianna Samu Design **page 287:** design: Donald Billinkoff AIA **pages 288–289:** *both* design: Baltimore Design Center **page 290:** *top* design: Eileen Katherine Boyd Interiors; *bottom* design: Sherrill Canet Design **pages 291–239:** *all* design: Lucianna Samu Design **page 303:** design: Baltimore Design Center

Have a home improvement, decorating, or gardening project?

Look for these and other fine

Creative Homeowner books

wherever books are sold.

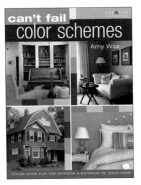

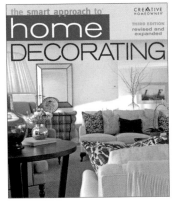
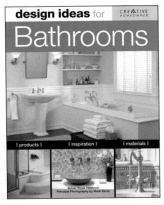
For more information and to order directly, go to
www.creativehomeowner.com